FAMILY TIME

Family Time

MARK & LINDSAY MELLUISH

Illustrated by
Helen Mahood

new wine international publishing

First published in Great Britain in 1999 by
new wine international publishing
PO Box 176, Berkhamsted, Herts, HP4 3FH, England.
ISBN 1 902977 00 9

First Edition 1999
10 9 8 7 6 5 4 3 2 1 0

Acknowledgements
All scripture quotations are taken from the Holy Bible,
New International Version, copyright © 1973, 1978, 1984
by International Bible Society. Used by permission of
Hodder and Stoughton Limited. All rights reserved.

A catalogue record for this book is available
from the British Library

Designed and produced for the publishers by
Gazelle Creative Productions,
Concorde House, Grenville Place,
Mill Hill, London NW7 3SA.

DEDICATION:

To Jessica, George, Callum and Beth.

CONTENTS

FOREWORD

Welcome to Family Time! What you will find within these pages is based on a set of talks we have put together as a Parenting Course in our church, St Paul's, Ealing. The course is aimed at those with children under 9 years old. We have four children aged 9, 6, 5 and 3. Not having personal experience of older children, we leave that to those who have already been through those later years! We do not go into the specific area of children with special needs, although many of the parents who have completed our courses have had children with special needs and have still found the material helpful.

We certainly don't hold ourselves up as model parents, even in the 'under 9' bracket — we have made so many mistakes and there will be many more yet! However, we are passionate about family life and what we want is for others to be passionate about it too. What we offer here is material to enthuse and envision those who want to be better parents. We have put the talks together in the form of a book so that the material could be made available more widely and provide resources and information to help you.

You may wish to use this book to help you run a Parenting Course in your own church or community. We have found that parents receive a great deal of encouragement and envisioning when they meet together to work through the material and enjoy group discussions with people in the same situation experiencing the same frustrations and joys. There is also the opportunity for ongoing support and friendship after the course has finished.

At the end of each chapter we have included discussion questions for each week and also suggestions as to what people can do at home between sessions.Also in the appendix at the back of the book entitled 'Running a Family Time course' you can read about how we run the course at St Paul's Ealing.

We want to acknowledge that over the 10 years or so that we have been parents, we have gleaned insight from a wide variety of resources and people, much of which we have used in putting this material together. Where this is the case we have given due credit. However, if there is anything that we have remembered and re-written unconsciously, we ask forgiveness.

We would also like to thank our wonderful church family at St Paul's for all their support and encouragement as we put together the course. We especially thank Lea Brown, Andrew and Nicola Holden, Jeremy and Julia Honer for all their help as we have lead the courses together, and all those who have been through it and offered their comments and ideas for improvement. Thank you to Helen Mahood for her wonderful illustrations. We feel so privileged to be part of this great church family with so much energy and enthusiasm for God and His ways.

And thank you too to our friends Keith and Caroline Wilson who have inspired and encouraged us in our own parenting, and who took us through a parenting course some years ago.

Finally, we would like to thank our parents for all they have given us and for their input into our own lives. And we want to thank especially our four children: Jessica, George, Callum and Beth (without whom we could never have written such a book!) for allowing us to use examples taken from our own family life and for bringing us so much joy and generally being such stars!

Mark and Lindsay Melluish
March 1999

1

WHERE DO WE BEGIN?

It is always with a healthy amount of fear and some trepidation that anyone attempts to write and present a parenting course. Lindsay and I are no different. After all, many of us have 'our ways' of doing things, and who are we to suggest other ways of approaching parenting?

However we believe that we do have something to share. I'm sure that you like us, have watched, with pain in your heart, as you have seen a child smacked in public, or shouted at in your local supermarket. Perhaps as you have seen these things happen you have thought, 'There must be a better way'?

We have sought to find a better way. It's not the only way and there may be people who think it not the best way. But it's the way in which we have chosen to parent, partly because it is based on what we read in the bible and partly because we have found that it works well.

What has happened to parenting?

Parenting varies tremendously according to cultural differences throughout the world and we are very aware that we only have one perspective, raising children in the West, where many things are available and on hand to help us. Yet even here parenting has gone through some fairly major revolutions in the last 30 years. Some of these changes are for the better, but some create new problems.

There has been a general demise of local communities, where families lived in close proximity for generations and everyone helped each other in the bringing up of babies and the discipline of children. Parenting skills used to be passed down, mistakes were learnt from and new discoveries were shared.

These family communities hardly exist any more. House prices, movement of industry, changes in the infrastructure and our educational system mean that we are all on the move. Many people leave home at 18 to go off to college, others leave in search of employment and so the break-down of communities spreads.

All this means that we often have to discover how to parent on our own. When we had our first child, we found that we learnt the most from our friends. What do you do when Jonny can't sleep? When do you start feeding solids? What is the best bedtime? How do you apply

for schools? When do you start giving pocket money? How much do you give? These are some of the questions that parents ask each other.

Many of us probably just assumed that we would know what to do when the baby came along. After all, we can work the Internet, use mobile phones and hold conferences throughout the world by telephone. We would know when the baby needed feeding, how to feed her and what to feed her, and of course we would soon work out the sleep issue that so many others were struggling with!

Yet the truth is, we have never met a situation like it before. This little bundle who came, so delightfully into our lives one day, this little bundle that was planned so carefully, delivered so professionally and dressed so perfectly, does not do as it is supposed to do. It does not respond like a machine, fit in with our busy lives, or behave like an adult who we can reason with; it's a child, full of life, who makes huge demands on our time.

The reality is that we have to learn how to parent. Of course everybody has a view on parenting. Some of the unhelpful comments we heard when we expressed our concerns about parenting for the first time were: 'It's a natural thing and you'll just know what to do when the baby comes along' or 'Parenting simply depends on the type of child you have'. Other comments were just as unhelpful 'Just you wait until they're two or three' or 'It's OK when they're young, just you wait until they're a little older'.

These comments simply filled us with a sense of panic, rather than feeling 'This is going to be one fantastic adventure!'

The common link in all of these statements, is the belief that the behaviour of children is completely dependent on anything other than parents. No account is taken of the huge part that we as parents play in determining who our children become.

Some unhelpful methods of parenting

What we believe is missing for so many parents is a thought- through methodology for parenting. In times gone by, this would have been passed from one generation to the next. A daughter would have been her mother's helper and the mother would have trained the daughter, not just in cooking, sewing and home making, but the time spent together would have trained the daughter in motherhood.

In a similar way a son would have worked with his father. A carpenter's son would learn the carpentry trade and his father would have apprenticed him. In doing this he would also have passed on life skills about marriage and relationships.

This doesn't mean that parents always got it right, but it did give children a model to follow. Today our models so often come from chat shows or magazines, or simply from a desperate need to find a way to survive.

Listed below are some of the survival methods which parents use. If we look hard we might see ourselves here from time to time.

Authoritarian Parent — This is where a parent seeks to

impose a standard upon a child which he expects the child to comply with but suspends that standard for himself. This of course is hypocritical, 'Do as I say, not as I do.' This comes down to little things such as putting your own seat belt on in the car as you expect your children to do, through to the larger issues such as putting others first in life.

Permissive Parent — This is where a parent lives to a standard but does not expect the child to do the same and makes excuses for him all the time, or just becomes

very tolerant of wrong behaviour. 'Oh they are only children what can you expect!'

I didn't turn out so badly — No methodology at all. e.g. 'My dad yelled at me. He used to knock me around once in a while. I didn't like it, but I turned out OK'. In this situation a parent realises that he has come from a background with no thought- out methodology. He realises that there was little consistency in decisions made, but he still chooses to follow the same example, however frustrating it may have been to him as a child.

Bribery and deals — We have seen this often where the parents creatively come up with deals to make children perform e.g. 'Clean your room and I'll treat you to an ice cream later on' or 'Stay quiet in the shopping trolley and I'll buy you some sweets at the end of the shop'. This is a very short-term approach. The point of appeal to the child is always going to be self-interest. The child is not taught to look out for the interests of others and learns nothing about his own heart and motives.

Emotionalism — This is parenting that plays on a child's sense of emotional well-being, e.g. 'I hate you', 'Go away', 'I don't want you', to make the child conform, or 'It really makes me sad when you say that. You are hurting me...' Or alternatively, shaming a child. Also long periods of isolation in 'Coventry'. Here a child is trained not to know, love and serve God, but merely to respond to the crippling fear of emotional privation. She may well ultimately be driven by a desire to please her parents and secure their approval. Or she may distance herself from them to avoid further hurt.

Punishment driven – This is control through threat of punishment, through negative experience of punishment, being hit, shouted at, or grounded, for example. Punishment is used as a tool for an end rather then as a corrective measure.

These approaches, though effective to some extent in amending outward behaviour, all miss the point of parenting as we see it in the Bible, where the emphasis seems to be on reaching the hearts of our children.

We believe we have the opportunity to influence and shape the future of our children's lives and this begins at birth. We can enjoy bringing up our children and hopefully other people can enjoy them as well.

The truth is that if we are to reach our children's hearts then ours have to be reached as well. We have to have hearts that want to follow God and his ways. Hearts that are not hard and critical but soft and open to learning, hearts that are humble and gentle. You will discover that many of the areas we cover in this book deal with our own lives as well as the lives of our children

There is no shortage of advice for parents at the moment, and courses abound offering different ways of bringing up your child. No course is perfect and we are sure you will want to think through what we are teaching here. However, our guidelines are based on a framework for parenting that we see in the Bible. Throughout the book we will be referring to God and to the Bible and we hope that you will be as excited as we are to discover the wisdom we can find in God's Word. We shall use the Bible as a basis for wisdom and as the foundation of what we hope to share with you.

It must be said that much of the material in this book challenges many of the things that we have grown up to accept as normal either through our own experience as adults or as children. Our aim is to help you reach a place that reflects God's desire for you as parents. We believe that we have a responsibility as Christians to seek to bring our children up in God's way.

We are not perfect parents, nor are we aiming to be because that is an impossible target. We are however looking to God to direct us in our parenting through the Bible. We are told many times in the Bible that if we follow the ways of God, He will bless us and our households. And we take that seriously.

Why use the Bible?

It's really a matter of relatives or absolutes. Either we have a firm foundation from which to base decisions (an absolute) or we have a life based on moving ground. Modern society promotes a very relativist attitude: do what suits you, I'll do what suits me. Jesus taught about this in the parable of the wise and foolish builder (Matthew 7:24–29). It was the wise man who built his house on the firm foundation, the foundation that had stood the test of time and the storms that blew over it. On the other hand the foolish man built his house on the sand, the moving ground. It may have been instant and quick to erect, but it did not last.

We are given children as a gift from God and we are to build structures into their lives that will prepare them for life. We believe the best teaching and value system we can place into our children's lives is the value system that God has given us in his Word. The teaching in the Bible refers to a way of life that is governed by God's guidelines. The Bible won't tell us that our children should share their toys and take turns when they are playing with other children, but it does talk about teaching our children about self-control, about respect and about care for others.

The Bible touches every area of life. If we use it to guide us and enlighten us it will help us with our parenting problems. So how does this work out?

Some of God's guidelines we find in Scripture are very specific. The ten commandments are very clear: 'You shall not steal', 'You shall not bear false witness' (i.e. always tell the truth) and 'Do not kill' are obvious examples. We are in no doubt about how we carry out these commands. These are things that we will want to place in our children's hearts and they will take them on board if they see us living them out as well.

Some things are less specific but still give us direction

in our parenting. 'Love your neighbour as yourself' is obviously a principle that Jesus lived out and one that we should encourage. Many young people today wear bands around their wrists with the initials, WWJD. This stands for What Would Jesus Do? and is a good practical way of putting principles into action.

It is the less specific guidelines or principles, that challenge us to think things through ourselves as we seek to determine what we should encourage our children to do. It isn't always black and white, sometimes our decision will depend on the circumstances.

For example, we have a telephone in our kitchen, next to the room where the children often play. Generally the children can play with complete freedom to make a noise and run about. However, if we should be speaking on the telephone, trying to hear the person on the other end of the line, that would change things. We would then expect the children to be quiet for those few moments until we had finished our call and then they could continue playing their noisy game! We could say 'no noisy games at all'. But that would be unnecessary. We need to judge according to the circumstances.

Another example. We lead a fairly busy church and after our worship has finished, hot tea and coffee is served. Often children run around while the adults are talking. There is no rule against this, but because of the hot coffee being served it is not a good idea for children to be running about! Therefore on a Sunday we encourage the children not to run in church. However, on a Thursday evening during the youth group, children can run in church. This is a different context. The legalist might say 'No running in church.' Our job as parents is to apply the principles we find in Scripture to the various situations we find ourselves in.

We all have a responsibility to look at the way we bring up our children. As they are a gift from God it is good to ask the giver how we should best care for these precious gifts.

The Bible is quite clear about this responsibility:

- Deut 6:4-9 v6 'These commandments that I give you today are to be upon your hearts. Impress them on your children.'

- Eph 6:4 'Fathers, do not exasperate your children; instead bring them up in the training and instruction of the Lord'

A child cannot always make good or helpful choices, so we as parents need to make them on our children's behalf. The Bible gives us a standard by which we can make wise choices on behalf of our children.

Our example!

We are called in Scripture to imitate Christ.

- Philippians 2:5 'Your attitude should be the same as that of Christ Jesus.'

Jesus' life was a model of putting others first – being other-focused.

- Mark 10:45 'For even the son of Man did not come to be served but to serve and to give His life as a ransom for many'

This also has to be the underlying motive behind our lives as Christians. We should be teaching our children to think of those around them. To care for others as others care for them. And we have to set the example. *Children may not be very good at listening to their elders, but they nearly always seem to find ways of imitating them.*

Our influence is CRUCIAL.

Statistics tell us that often patterns of behaviour are repeated in families. This is of course not always the case and we believe that bad patterns of behaviour are broken when people meet with Jesus. However just as we see and hear ourselves in the little things our children say and do, so we will also see in them a clearer reflection of our lives as they grow up.

During the first few years of our children's lives, their parents are the heroes. Children want to be like their parents. Nothing matters more to them than what their parents think. If we are honest and kind, they will be honest and kind. If we are rude and arrogant, they are likely to be rude and arrogant.

I'm sure that you, like us, have heard or watched with embarrassment as your children have imitated you in public. We hear them speaking as we do. We watch them acting as we do, and responding as we do. *It is unreasonable to expect a child to listen to your advice and ignore your example.*

As parents we are given the joy and responsibility of being a role model for our children. **We reproduce who we are not, what we say!** It is beyond doubt that the way we parent our children is the single most crucial factor in determining who they become. We must be the kind of person we want our children to become.

This means we have to be: considerate drivers; to return things we borrow; to put the cheese we don't want back on the cheese counter at the supermarket rather than leaving it with the toilet rolls! Our children pointed out to us that although we expected them to make their beds before coming down stairs for breakfast in the morning, we didn't always make ours. So things had to change! In the same way we have to teach our children to tidy their own bedrooms, hang up their own clothes and so

on! We have to teach them to think of others first. And we have to do the same. This can be very challenging.

There are ways in which we can help our children to be other-focused and we will be covering this in more detail later. However getting our children to do jobs which serve the whole family will encourage them to think of others. Laying the table, for example, encourages selflessness. This is in contrast to asking them to do only those jobs which benefit themselves, such as making their own bed or tidying up their toys.

Where the rubber first hits the road!

'Values are caught and taught!'

- Deuteronomy 6:4–9 v6 'These commandments that I give you today are to be upon your hearts. Impress them on your children.'

The process begins with the parents. We need first to check out our own hearts and then go on to reach our children's hearts. The aim is for any outward change in behaviour to be the result of an inner change of heart.

- Proverbs 4:23 'Above all else, guard your heart, for it is the well spring of life'

The heart is a well from which all the issues of life flow. This simply means that the way a person lives is an expression of his heart.

When God wanted to appoint a new king over Israel; He sent Samuel to Bethlehem to find the sons of Jesse. Samuel arrived and prepared to make a sacrifice to the Lord to which he invited Jesse and his sons. As Eliab approached, Samuel thought this must be the one that God wants to make king for he was strong and handsome. But God had another in mind and He said to Samuel...

- 1 Samuel 16:7 'Do not consider his appearance or his height, for I have rejected him. The Lord does not look at the things man looks at. Man looks at the outward appearance, but the Lord looks at the heart'

God is interested in our hearts and the hearts of our children. If we are to follow the pattern of God then we too should be interested in our children's hearts not just their behaviour.

Parents often get side tracked with behaviour. If our goal in discipline is changed behaviour then it is easy to understand why this happens. Bad behaviour calls for correction and attention. However in trying to correct the behaviour it is easy to overlook the reason for the behaviour.

The way our children behave — the things they say and do — reflects their hearts. If we are to help our children to grow up and live life to the full, then we have to be concerned with the attitudes of heart that drive their behaviour. We can all train our children to do certain things in robot-like ways, but we need to to help them to understand the reasons why, so that they themselves can have hearts which are motivated to do the right thing.

So it might be that you have a rule that the children have to tidy up all the toys before they go to bed. Such a rule is a good one. But if you want them to learn about being responsible talk with them about it. They need to tidy their toys because they made the mess, so why should their mum or dad clear up after them?

Obviously there is a point up to which children won't understand 'why' and will just have to live with the instruction to do as mum or dad says, but after about the age of three we must begin to explain the moral reasons behind the practical instruction. The result of this is that obedience becomes attractive to a child because he understands what is going on and so is less frustrated with life.

Teaching our children the ways of God doesn't just affect behaviour

Teaching our children the ways of God affects the whole person. Think about self-control for example. Self-control is one of the fruits of the Spirit, along with love, joy, peace, patience, gentleness, faithfulness, kindness and goodness. Self-control is a product of training the heart.

A major influence in our society is the intellectual stimulation of our children. Playgroups are scrutinised before we send our children there and many people pay for groups that will push their child on. Self-control is perhaps less highly rated, yet is as valuable as any good play-school or nursery and will have lasting benefits which will be just as influential and effective, if not more so in the long term.

Ask yourself how self-control manifests itself. It gives the ability to sit, to focus the mind, to concentrate for longer periods of time. This and other fruits of the Spirit are things which if your child has them can only help them in their education process.

When we train the heart of a child we train the whole child.

The Bible shows us how to parent. It provides us with a framework for our lives, which we in turn can impress on our children.

In this book we hope you will find ideas that challenge, basic principles and skills that every parent will need and new horizons you can reach for. We do not provide for every eventuality, neither are we able to cover every aspect of parenting. But we do promise you an adventure that is exciting, rewarding and fun.

BIBLE VERSES USED IN THIS CHAPTER

Matthew 7:24-29
Exodus 20:1-17
Mark 12:31
Deuteronomy 6:4-9
Ephesians 6:4
Philippians 2:5
Mark 10:45
Proverbs 4:23
1 Samuel 16:7

Questions for discussion groups

1 What do you feel about the idea of reaching the hearts of our children as a foundation for parenting?

2 Many of us have, I'm sure, been side-tracked with behaviour when issues of the heart are clearly so much more important. What are the benefits of focusing on the heart rather than on behaviour?

3 Have you come accross any of the unhelpful methods of parenting mentioned, either in yourself or in your own parents? Can you think of any other common unhelpful ways of disciplining and bringing up children?

4 As we've heard, a legalist makes a rule and sticks to it regardless of the circumstances (e.g. no noisy games in the playroom). What benefits do you think will come from making parenting decisions according to the circumstances?

Application points...

1 Try providing the reason why when you ask your child to do something, if you don't do it already, and note the response.

2 Try to consider the circumstances before making parenting decisions this week. See if it helps you to parent more fairly.

3 In the light of today's material, review honestly the example that you set to your children now or if your children are very young (or haven't yet arrived) the example you hope to set in the future.

2

THOSE WHOM GOD HAS JOINED TOGETHER...

The family is the primary social unit of society, and it is one worth protecting and keeping. And yet, as we look at the world around us, we see families who are being driven apart by the pressures of work, large mortgages, inflated material needs. We see people, who for various reasons are working longer hours. With the availability of pre-prepared meals, the microwave and the dishwasher it is possible to spend far less time at home than once would have been feasible.

Inevitably this type of lifestyle has a knock-on effect where the family is concerned. For family relationships to grow, those families need to spend time together. Without time together families become fragmented. Many people don't realise it is happening, until one day it strikes them that the quality of their family life is not what they had hoped for when they first set out. They find themselves asking, 'What happened? How did it go wrong?' So often by then it is too late.

We hope that as you read this book you will have an opportunity to look at your family life and to take steps to ensure that you don't get to that position. And perhaps one of the most important areas to focus on in terms of strengthening our family units is that of our relationship with our husband or wife, the father or mother of our children. This is the focus of this chapter. We shall consider the role of the marriage relationship within our families and also what we can do to help keep it in good order. If you're parenting alone, please don't skip this part, believing that it doesn't affect you. We have included some pointers for you and we do believe that much, of what we have to say here will still be relevant in your situation.

The husband and wife relationship[1]

A man called Theodore Hesberg once said, 'The most important thing a father can do for his children is to love their mother.' And a brief look into the opening chapters of the Bible helps shed some light on what he meant as we read in them what we believe to be God's ideal for the family unit.

In Genesis chapter 2 we read of how God created man and then very quickly decided 'It is not good for man to be alone.' Man was surrounded by animals and had a perfect, unspoilt relationship with God but he was still deemed, by God, to be 'alone'. What he needed was an intimate relationship with one of his own kind, someone with whom he could share life intimately at every level — spiritually, socially, emotionally and physically.

And so God decided to 'make a suitable helper for him', a helper being someone who would complete and compliment the man in every way. And He created the woman and brought her to the man and united the two. In Genesis 2:24 we read: 'For this reason a man shall leave his father and his mother and be joined to his wife; and they shall become one flesh.' So we see that God's purpose for marriage and in creating woman was to provide a companion for man, someone with whom he could share his life. This was why marriage, the one-flesh union, was designed. And as we have seen, the 'one-flesh' concept refers to more than just physical oneness: it is emotional and physical as well and in addition, it is a social oneness. Through marriage, husband and wife leave their parental homes and take on a new identity in the community as a unit.

Throughout Scripture we see marriage as an institution which is highly valued and so much so that Jesus' relationship with His church is even likened to that of a bridegroom with his bride (Ephesians 5:25).

And in the creation story, it seems that God viewed the union of the woman with the man as His ultimate achievement because once He had completed it and seen that it was 'very good', He rested. (Genesis 1:27–31)

And it's interesting that even though they had no children as yet — they came along later — God looked upon the coming together of the man and woman as 'very good.' And this is significant for us because it conveys the message that a man and woman who are married to one another are complete.

Now of course we love our children and life would be dismal without them. But we do well to remember that long long ago, before the children came along, the two of us when we married one another were seen by God as 'very good'. Contrary to what we are often encouraged to believe, we didn't have to wait to have an allotted number of children before being considered a complete family. As husband and wife we were already complete. When the children arrived, our family increased in size, but they didn't make us any more complete.

So how does all this affect us now? It means that, if we are married and living with our husband or wife, even though we have children, our relationship with our partner takes first place in the family. In fact the quality of all the relationships in the family and also the security of our children will depend on the quality of their mum and dad's marriage. And if that is the case, it follows that our marriage relationship must take priority in the family. We need to take pains to make sure that we are doing all that is within our power to make our marriages the best they can possibly be, and not just for us but for the sake of our children.

So often parents see their function to be first and foremost to provide for the needs of their children. So often we unwittingly ignore the needs of our husband or wife because we are preoccupied with the children. So often our husbands or wives get us at the tail end of the day when we are tired and fit only to fall asleep on the sofa. And more often than not all this is done with the best of intentions — to do the best for our children. Ironically, though, the result is that so often a marriage that began with great promise, loses all its vitality because it is starved of nourishment and the children miss out on one of the best gifts you can give them. Nothing we can buy or do for our children is more important than showing them that their mum and dad love and value one another and that together we lead the family, under God. And it's as we do this that harmony, order and structure can prevail in our families and in society as well.

If you are parenting alone, you may be asking yourself where all this leaves you in your situation. We believe that there is a great deal which you can draw from all this.

First of all, we all, regardless of our situation, need to understand the biblical perspective on marriage and the family. It's something we'll all want to pass on to our children so that they will get a grasp of God's ideal for the family, even if it's not their experience here and now.

Also, over 36% of marriages involve at least one partner who has been married before and in 17% of marriages both partners have been married before. It will be helpful to have a biblical understanding of marriage in any future reconciliation or remarriage.

And perhaps most importantly, if you're parenting on your own it is still important to have a relationship that takes priority over the other relationships in the family. Where a husband or wife is absent, your relationship with God can fill that gap. Isaiah 54:5 says, 'For your Maker is your husband' and Psalm 68:5 says God is 'A Father to the fatherless.' These verses will become especially significant for you if you're on your own and God will give you extra strength as you depend on him for your needs.

Let your children know how important your relationship with God is. Let them draw security from seeing you spending time with God and allow the strength which you draw from Him to be a source of stability and quality in your relationships both inside and outside the family. There are other benefits, too, of developing your relationship with God in this special way. These will become clearer as we move onto our next section.

Child-focused parenting

As soon as you had your first child, you may have begun to take much more of an interest in how your friends, family and work colleagues bring up their children. And you will have had your own ideas about what you saw and will have decided either that that was definitely not how you were going to do it, or you admired what they did and wanted to build some of it into your own family life. In this section we look at one particular approach to family life, child-focused parenting.

Parents for whom everything revolves around the children, who believe that their children are the focus of life itself and who seek to adapt the world to suit their children rather than teaching their children to adapt to their world are child-focused. Often we do it in the name of good parenting and sometimes through external pressure. When our first child was born, our inclination was to continue to give time to one another. However, so much of what we read and heard seemed to suggest that

we should no longer expect to have any time for each other, and we almost felt guilty for putting the baby in her cot and spending time alone together!

We may know of families that seem to be child-focused and we may even think at times we have fallen into it ourselves. We have probably all done it at one time or another.

Child-focused parenting can adversely affect family life in several ways:

— Firstly, the Bible says in Mark 10:9, 'what God has joined together, let not man separate.' If we allow our children always to be our priority, our focus shifts away from our partner and we then no longer fulfil our role as husband or wife and instead we bury ourselves in the role of mum or dad where we can feel less exposed and accountable.

— If you are parenting alone, to be child-focused can allow your child as he or she gets older to take the place of a husband or wife. In this way the child becomes an equal and a friend to mum or dad — a relationship which no child should be expected to cope with. It is also confusing for the child because it is difficult to learn to respect and obey mum and dad when the relationship is such that he or she is treated as an equal.

— In addition, to be child-focused gives a child the feeling that he is self-reliant, with the attitude 'I don't need anybody else, I can manage on my own.' It gives the child the feeling that because everything revolves around him he doesn't need to invest in relationships other than those that will be of benefit to him personally. For relationships within and outside the family to be strong and healthy, we all need to invest in them, we need to be interdependent. Our children need to know that other people matter, regardless of whether we will always gain personally from maintaining a relationship with them. You may be able to think of families yourself where the children are positively encouraged to look out for other people and to consider their feelings. Such children often talk easily with other adults and children and have an ability to make those people feel valued even though they might not know them very well at all.

— Parents who are child-focused often afford their child more freedom than he can cope with and give him a false self-sufficiency. Children who have freedom given to them before they have acquired the self-control to manage it will likely come a cropper. In our church on a Sunday morning we often have a slot when we have children's songs and all the children go up to the front to sing them. And in our family this has been something that has become a kind of privilege that comes with age, around about $2^1/_2$ years old. This is because we have only allowed our children to go to the front once we knew that they were mature enough to join in and not get themselves into trouble by running around or messing about or climbing all over each other! We have sought to give them the freedom once we know they can cope with it.

— Finally, those who are child-focused often find it difficult to find and maintain a standard for their children and are often having to adapt any such standard rather than face addressing the behaviour of their child.

What we are saying then, is that if a child learns that he is at the centre of the family he will likely be self-centred and will have difficulty in making relationships both inside and outside of the family unit. He will tend to be a taker and not a giver. On the other hand, a child who sees his place in the family more as a member of a team will be confident and secure in where he fits in. He will therefore make relationships naturally and comfortably, giving as well as receiving and growing up knowing the importance of investing in family relationships and caring for others.

How can we make the marriage relationship a priority and guard against child-focused parenting?

— Remember, life doesn't stop when you have children. It changes but it doesn't stop. Just because you become a father or mother, don't stop being a sister, brother, friend, daughter, son and above all... a husband or wife.

— When you arrive home, make a point of saying hello to your husband or wife. Make it a priority to do that first before attending to the clamouring children, so

that everyone knows that mum and dad matter to each other. If you are parenting alone, ask your family and friends and particularly your own parents to make a point of greeting you first when they arrive before making a fuss of the children. Explain to them that you want the children to see you valuing other close relationships as well as your relationship with them.

— Try to take time to talk to your husband or wife every day without interruptions — and when the children are around to see, not after they are in bed! They might object at first but soon they will grow to enjoy seeing you enjoying time with each other and will feel more secure as a result.

— Do something together as husband and wife, say, once a week. Go to the cinema, go out for a walk, a meal, have a take-away with a video, play tennis. Have a weekend away once in a while. Do something you both enjoy but above all, do it together without the children and let them know why you're doing it: because you enjoy being together!

— If you are parenting alone make sure you have 10-15 minutes with God, when the children are awake, and let them know that this is a priority for you as you and He lead the family together. They will draw security from this and look forward to your time spent with God once they understand it. They might even remind you if you forget!

— Use your home to serve other people. Entertain as a family to help each other to work as a team and to help the children to learn to look out for other people. We often entertain on a Sunday lunchtime and sometimes we might ask the children who they think would enjoy an invitation to lunch. Having decided together who to invite we can all take a share in entertaining those people and giving them, hopefully, a good time!

How can I learn to say, 'I love you'?[2]

As we've said so far in this chapter, we believe that children who are assured of their parents' love for one another will have greater confidence in their parents' love for them and in turn this sense of being loved can then enhance and strengthen other relationships.

Love is the hallmark of the Christian. John 13:35 says, 'All men will know that you are my disciples if you love one another.' God wants us to love one another so that the world will know that we belong to Him. And Jesus is our example in this, as in the previous verse He says, 'A new command I give you. Love one another. As I have loved you so you must love one another.'

But, like most things that are worth having, love doesn't come easily and we actually have to learn how to love. We have to learn how to give it and how to receive it because love will never be real unless it is demonstrated by the lover and received by the loved. Simply to know in our head that we love someone is useless because it means nothing to that person. God has created us with the capacity both to feel loved and more importantly to choose to demonstrate it. And we have to learn to express that love so that the person it is directed at actually feels loved.

How often have we tried to show our love for our partner or our children only for our efforts to be misinterpreted? Or vice versa. We long for our partner or children to show their love and at the same time completely misunderstand the things they are doing out of love for us.

Thinking specifically of the marriage relationship for a moment, why is it that in spite of the vast number of magazines, television programmes, books and seminars that abound on the subject of romantic love, so often the complaint comes that it is difficult to keep love alive after the wedding?

It seems that inside each of us there is an invisible

al love tank' which is waiting to be filled with hat tank is constantly on empty, our marriage feless. We will have no desire to give out love to our partner because we don't feel loved ourselves. We become withdrawn, isolated, maybe critical. If the tank is full, on the other hand, the marriage becomes alive and the emotional climate is such that differences and conflicts can be resolved and the couple can live in peace and harmony in the confidence that he or she is truly loved by their partner.

The question is, why is it that so often our love tanks are on empty; why do we sometimes not truly feel loved? One answer is this: people are different. And different people speak different love languages.

Have you ever had the experience of going on holiday abroad to a country where you don't know the language? How awkward it can be when a native comes up to you and begins to speak to you. You probably shake your head, gesticulate and perhaps speak very loudly and slowly in English but your efforts are largely in vain.

If you do find someone who can speak English it's as though a light has been switched on, and the conversation flows because you understand one another and you're both comfortable speaking your native or primary language.

In the area of love it's similar. Your emotional love language and the language of your husband or wife or children may be as different as English from German, or French, or even Chinese. If your partner speaks only Chinese, you may try as hard as you can to express your love in English but it will never be received. Similarly, you might try to show love to your wife by telling her how beautiful she is, that you love her, that you are proud of her. But if she doesn't understand that language she won't receive it as love. Maybe she is looking for you to show her love by holding her and touching her. She may be thinking that because you don't do those things, you don't love her.

John Gray in his book 'Men are from Mars, Women are from Venus' says this: 'We mistakenly assume that if our partners love us they will react and behave in certain ways — the ways we react and behave when we love someone. This attitude sets us up to be disappointed again and again and prevents us from taking the necessary time to communicate lovingly about our differences.'[3]

We must be willing to learn our partner's primary love language if we are to be effective communicators of love. In this next section, we're going to look at how this

works out in practice. And whilst we have drawn examples largely from the marriage relationship, bear in mind, especially if you are parenting alone, that these love languages apply not only to husbands and wives but to children and close friends as well.

The five love languages

There are five love languages. Within those languages there may be a number of dialects and the number of ways to express love within a love language is limited only by one's imagination. The important thing is to speak the love language of your partner. So what are they?

1 Words of affirmation

One way of expressing love is to use words which build up (1 Thessalonians 4:18 and 5:11). Genuine *verbal compliments or words of appreciation* are powerful communicators of love. They are best expressed in simple, straightforward statements of affirmation such as, 'You look great in that dress' or 'Thanks for sorting out a babysitter for tonight. I really appreciate it' or 'The house is spotless! You must have worked really hard on it.'

Can you imagine what would happen to the emotional climate of a marriage if the husband and wife heard such words of affirmation regularly? I (Lindsay) know that personally, I am far more motivated if I am complimented than if I am nagged. And I know from experience that Mark is the same!

Another way of giving affirmation is to use encouraging words. Many of us lack confidence and could achieve so much more in life if we had someone to encourage us and make us believe we can do what we want to do.

So, for example, if your husband says he is thinking of going to Weight Watchers once the warmer weather arrives, you could either say, 'At last! I've been hoping you'd do that for years!' Or you could say, 'Good for you. I'm sure you'll do well because you're always so determined once you set your mind on something. Maybe I could do it with you and we could change what we eat to suit your diet. We'll probably both feel better for it.'

Words like this might not come easily at first, especially if you're not used to it. But dare to try it and see what a difference it makes! I can speak personally (Lindsay) and say that I know I have achieved so much more in life because I have a husband who has been willing to encourage me every step of the way. What a great gift to give to a husband or wife who responds to words of encouragement!

Another way of speaking words of affirmation is to speak kind words. If someone is ranting and raving at you and you choose to respond lovingly with kind, gentle words, you will know how the heat is taken out of the situation. Recently, I was in the Post Office and inadvertently went to a counter that was closed. The clerk was very grumpy with me and huffed and puffed pointing to the 'closed' sign. I apologised not just once but intermittently throughout my dealings with him. By the end he had completely changed his attitude and assured me that it had been no trouble and it wasn't my fault at all!

The Bible says in Proverbs, 'A gentle answer turns away wrath'. Once the anger has gone we can seek to discover why our partner is upset and to resolve the problem.

Another way of speaking words of affirmation is to make your requests humbly, rather than making demands. 'You know that fruit cake you sometimes make? Would it be possible to have one this weekend? I love that cake.' What a great way of affirming her but also letting her know gently what you like and showing her how to love you.

So, if your husband or wife responds to words of affirmation, make a conscious effort to accumulate things you can say to affirm him. Try praising him to others

when he is not present too. It will be sure to filter back to him and he'll love it.

2 Quality Time

Quality time is giving someone your undivided attention. That means, not sitting with half an eye on the football as your wife tells you how hurt she was this evening that you didn't notice her new hairstyle — but rather sitting on the sofa with the TV off, talking; or going for a walk together; or going out for a meal together. The key word is *together*. For some it might not have to involve talking, quality time might be just playing tennis together for example, going shopping, visiting antique fairs, having a picnic. And the great thing about these sorts of things is that they provide a memory bank of things to draw from in the years ahead.

Quality time may need working at! In our home quality time often means going shopping together. Now for some reason I (Mark) don't enjoy shopping. But Lindsay does. So often on a Tuesday, our day off together Lindsay will suggest we go shopping. I've given up asking what for as it often seems unimportant, but the time spent together in a joint activity is important. I have also learnt how to find good coffee shops and lunch stops!

For most people whose primary love language is quality time, talking will be important. So your wife will want to know that if you're loving her by giving her quality time and conversation, then you will listen sympathetically to what she has to say and respond by asking the sort of questions which show you have understood her.

A lady came to us some while back and said that her husband was wonderful in so many ways, so helpful around the home, was always tidying up and doing the odd jobs that were needed. 'But', she said, 'if only he would read about these Love Languages he might realise that he is completely missing the point when it comes to what makes me feel loved. I just long for quality time with him.'

Lindsay is not a television person. In fact I don't think that she ever switches it on unless there is a certain film or programme on that she wants to watch. On the other hand, I will often come in from a busy evening out and to help unwind after the busyness of the day and the different problems that have come my way, I will often turn on the television. Generally I hope to catch the news but will also see if there is anything worth watching for half an hour or so. The problem when I do this is that I get totally engrossed in the programme I choose to watch. Lindsay will often come and sit with me and rather than have the television on will want to talk about the day. I have had to learn that any programme or film is not as important (however much I am into it!) as switching off the television in order to talk together at the end of the day.

If you are not really a quality time person, and your

partner is, there are certain things you may need to learn: to listen, to maintain eye contact when your spouse is talking, to listen for feelings, to watch body language, and not to interrupt! And you might also need to learn to share your own feelings. If your wife 'wishes you would talk more', she is looking for intimacy in conversation and that involves revealing yourself as well as listening.

If your wife's primary love language is quality time, and specifically conversation, her emotional love tank will never be filled until you tell her your thoughts and feelings. This might not come easily to you, especially if you grew up in the kind of home where feelings were not shared, or if you have a strong, silent personality and you are married to a chatterbox. But it'll be worth it.

3 *Receiving gifts*

A gift is a visual symbol of the fact that someone remembered you when you weren't there. It doesn't matter if it didn't cost much. What matters is that receiving it is an expression of love.

These tangible symbols of love are more important to some people than to others. Think for example of your wedding ring, if you have one. Is it important to you or would you be just as happy not to have one? When we got married, Mark decided he didn't want a wedding ring. It wasn't important to him. For me (Lindsay), on the other hand, my wedding ring is so important that I have never even removed it from my finger. If receiving gifts is one of your primary love languages, the gifts that your husband has given you over the years will probably be very important to you.

Our oldest daughter is a great gift-giver. When she goes out for the day she always comes home laden with presents for not only the immediate family but for the lodgers as well. And she puts great value on the things she has been given. Her favourite teddy was given to her as a baby by her much-loved cousins and, old and shabby as he is, she takes him to bed every night. She said to me just recently how much teddy means, and the more so because he is so old and has lost his colour.

If your partner's primary love language is receiving gifts, and if giving doesn't come naturally you can easily become a proficient gift-giver. Begin by making a list of all the presents your partner has been excited about receiving over the years and this will show you the sorts of gifts to go for. If you need help, ask her best friend.

If you haven't been used to spending money on gifts, you may need to change your attitude to money and learn to see spending money as an expression of love. This will be the best investment you could make.

4 Acts of Service

The Bible says 'love with actions and in truth' (1 John 3:18). Jesus gave an example of acts of service when He washed His disciples' feet. The roads were dusty and people's feet got dirty in their sandals and it was customary for the servants to wash guests' feet when they arrived. Jesus gave the disciples an example of how to show love by taking a basin and a towel and washing their feet. He then encouraged them to do the same. Paul, too, said 'Serve one another in love' (Galatians 5:13)

Love is a *choice*. When we choose to do something for our partner or our children that we know they would like us to do, we are showing them love in action.

Recently I (Mark) had an opportunity to show my love for Lindsay through an 'Act of Service' in our home. Lindsay was going away for a couple of days to stay with a girlfriend in Cheltenham. So the day before she was due to go I washed the car, filled it with petrol, checked the tyre pressures and topped up the windscreen washer bottle. Doing something that is not asked for but shows in a special way that you care for your partner's every need is an Act of Service

You could try cooking a meal, taking the rubbish out,

sweeping the kitchen floor, changing a nappy, cleaning the windows, cleaning out the hamster, mowing the lawn, vacuuming, hanging the washing out, emptying the dishwasher. All these things, if they are not your usual job and so if done unexpectedly, can be expressions of love if done with thought and with a positive spirit.

Lindsay is not a morning person and I know that if I get out of bed five minutes earlier than usual and make her a cup of tea to help her discover that it's daytime it is greatly appreciated. I am acting in love. In the same way if I am able to help with cooking a meal whilst Lindsay is busy with homework, ballet, piano and the many other after school activities, then this is engaging in an act of service, simply because in our home, this is not a job that I usually do.

If your partner's primary love language is acts of service, their love tank will soon fill up as you show them love in action. The important thing is to do those things which you know they want you to do and to do them not because you are coerced but because you choose to.

5 Physical touch

We all know that physical touch is a way of communicating emotional love. We know that babies and children who receive plenty of hugs and kisses develop a healthier emotional life than those who are left without.

We know too that physical touch is a powerful vehicle for communicating marital love. Holding hands, hugging, kissing and making love are all ways of communicating emotional love to one's partner. For some people, physical touch is their primary love language. Without it they feel unloved. With it their love tank is filled and they feel secure in the love of their spouse.

As we've said, men are different from women. In his book 'His needs, her needs', Willard F Harley lists the five chief needs of men and the five chief needs of women (taken from a survey). Perhaps surprisingly, neither list contained anything at all that was on the other and it also showed that for many men physical touch is very high on their list of priorities. It goes without saying then that if that is the case we women need to be making love to our husbands. It needs to be high on our agendas. Sex for lots of men is like quality time for lots of women. Without it they just don't feel loved. Without it their love tank will never be full.

So, love touches may be explicit such as in the act of making love. Or they may be implicit and require only a moment such as a hand on the shoulder as you pour a coffee, or a kiss as you pass each other in the kitchen. If you didn't grow up in a touchy family this might not come easily to you at first but if you discover that physical touch is your partner's primary love language you can soon learn to use your imagination to find ways to express love.

Your children and their love languages

Most parents love their children and equally they want their children to feel they are loved. If you can discover your child's primary love language you will be at a distinct advantage in loving your child in a way that makes him *feel* loved as well as just knowing you love him.

When children are little it is difficult to know what is their primary love language so pour on all five and you are bound to be right! But if you watch them you can discover it early.

— If your child is always making and wrapping presents for you and responds very positively when given a gift, Receiving Gifts may be his primary love language. He gives because he likes to receive. If so, gifts don't have to be expensive or cost anything at all. The fact that they are 'given' will be enough to fill the tank!

— If your child runs to you and jumps on your lap when you arrive and strokes your hair and wants to be touched, his primary love language may be Physical Touch. If so, give him plenty of hugs and kisses, as many as he can take!

— If your child always comes and shows you things he has written, or drawn and looks for praise or responds very positively when his behaviour is praised, then words of affirmation may be his primary love language. If so, give him lots of encouragement. Praise his successes rather than highlighting his failures (which would of course go for all children!).

— All children need quality time, some more than others. What you can do is enter into their interests, watch them playing sport, listen to them practising the piano, give them the time they are looking for. If you do this when they are young, the chances are they will allow you to spend time with them in their adolescent years and beyond.

— If your child is often very grateful for the things you do for him and often offering to help you, his primary love language may be Acts of Service. Helping him to mend his bicycle or a toy will mean a lot to him and help to fill his tank.

You can discover more about your children's love languages if you read Gary Chapman's book 'The Five Love Languages of Children.' (See acknowledgements)

How can we discover our own primary love language?

Ask yourself these questions:

— What makes you feel most loved by your partner? What do you desire above all else?

— What does your partner do or say that hurts you? If criticism springs to mind maybe your primary love language is Words of Affirmation.

— What have you most requested of your partner? The thing you most request is probably the thing that would most make you feel loved

— How do you most express love to your partner?

Often we express love in the way we would like it expressed to us.

Take time to work out your primary love language and then work out the order of the other four. Then try to work out the order for your partner and for your children. Then see the difference it makes to your family life as you seek to put love into action!

BIBLE VERSES USED IN THIS CHAPTER

Genesis 2:18 and 2:24
Ephesians 5:25
Genesis 1:27-31
Isaiah 54:5
Psalm 68:5
Mark 10:9
John 13:35
1 Thessalonians 4:8 and 5:11
Proverbs 15:1
1 John 3:18
Galatians 5:13

Acknowledgements

1 The first part of this chapter, the section on the husband and wife relationship and child-centred parenting is an adaptation of Chapter 3 of *Growing Kids God's Way* by Gary & Ann Marie Ezzo, Growing Families International Press, 1993.
2 For a more thorough explanation of this topic refer to *The Five Love Languages* by Gary Chapman Northfield Publishing, Chicago, 1995.
3 *Men are from Mars, Women are from Venus* by John Gray, Harper Collins inc, 1992
4 *The Five Love Languages of Children* by Gary Chapman & Ross Campbell, MD, Northfields Publishing, 1997

Recommended reading for this chapter:

The Five Love Languages by Gary Chapman, Northfield Publishing
Loving against the odds by Rob Parsons, Hodder & Stoughton

Questions for discussion groups

1 What is a family? Some might say that a family is established once two adults come together and have children. What does the Bible say a family is?

2 Having looked at child-focused parenting and its effects, can you think of real life examples of this, either from your own personal experience as a child or from what you have noticed around you?

3 Gary Chapman in *The Five Love Languages* says that love is a choice. What does he mean?

Application points...

1 Consider whether as a family you are too child-focused. List some things you could do to guard against it.

2 This week when you come home in the evening, try spending 15 minutes talking together before taking time with the children. Note your children's responses.

3 Try to work out your children's priority order for the love languages. If they are old enough, discuss it with them and see whether they can rank your love languages and their own.

3

MAKE HAY... WHILE THE SUN SHINES

In chapter 1 we introduced the aim that we feel is important to hold onto in our parenting; to reach our children's hearts in order that we might enable them ultimately to live a life which honours God.

In this chapter we look at an area which is key if we are to be in any way effective in our aim. If we hope to train and shape our children in such a way that they take on board for themselves the things we teach them, then it is vital that our relationships with them are strong, that channels of communication are always open and most important of all that our children know we love them. So we're going to look at some practical things we can do to build those relationships with our children.

The time as fathers and mothers when we have most influence and opportunity to shape and guide our children's lives is when they are very young — and it is a relatively short period, say 10–12 years. How many of us I wonder have said to ourselves 'I can't believe how quickly they are growing up!'?

We are given an opportunity now to involve ourselves in the lives of our children. Now is the time to build and secure relationships with them for life. Now is the time to lay firm foundations. The time spent in relationship now will probably last for life.

Time is precious

Gladys Knight and the Pips sang a song called 'The Way We Were'. It went something like this,

'The good old days the good old days. The winters were warmer, the days were brighter, the smiles were broader, but you know, just as bad as we think today is, these will be the good old days for our children'

What will stick in our children's minds as they look back in years to come? Will they remember that Mum often had so much to do that it was rare for her to come and play a game or that Dad was often caught up at work? Or will have they have memories of really good times, of Mum and Dad getting involved with them at every opportunity? We can make these the 'really good old days' for our children if we so choose. But we have to make the time. We have to use each day wisely. To communicate with children is to be there. To be there for our children is to communicate their worth and preciousness. It's so easy to fall into the trap of thinking that today is busy but it's a one-off and tomorrow will be easier; tomorrow there'll be more time, tomorrow I'll be there. The best thing parents can spend on children is time, not money.

In no time at all we'll be left wondering how they grew up so quickly. No more voices shouting 'Mummy, will you come and buy something from our shop?' or 'Daddy, please would you get my drum down from that high shelf?' No more dirty hand marks up the stairs, no more treading on bits of Lego in your bare feet as you visit the bathroom in the middle of the night. No more 'Can you make me a hat Daddy?'

No longer will we hear ourselves saying for the umpteenth time 'I'll be there in a minute...' or 'I'll just...' or 'I don't want to hear any more about it!' or 'Not now!'

These days will be over in what will seem like a twinkling.

The ironing, the vacuuming, the car, the fitness club, the local pub, the football team, the squash club or whatever it is that's important to us will always be there. Our children won't. But if we make time for them now while we have the *choice*, the chances are much higher that they'll make time for us when it's their turn to choose.

So let's make the most of it now! Let's not miss our opportunity. We all have the same amount of time each day. We can't save time, we can only spend it and we have to make choices as to how we spend the time God has given us.

Time — quantity or quality?

The expression 'quality time' has become a very fashionable one in recent years. This probably has something to do with the increasingly frenetic lives that some of us live as families which means that often time together gets squeezed out. The result is that the time we do spend together becomes all the more precious and so perhaps we call it 'quality time' in the hope that it will be just that!

It has become 'the thing' to work on an assumption that quality is better than quantity. The 'quality time person' may not have much time but what they do have they will make the most of. The 'quantity time person', on the other hand, thinks that just by being around, by being visible, that somehow communication is happening.

But we all know the difference between being around physically but not emotionally. Our physical presence does not indicate our commitment to someone. And equally we know that just because people are talking about quality time doesn't mean it is a reality and there are still many children who crave quality time even though their parents love them to bits.

'The problem with communicating with children is that you have to put in a lot of quantity so that the quality can really happen'[1]

If we are to build an open, honest, trusting relationship with our children in which they're able to come to us with confidence whatever the problem and whatever their age, we'll need to invest time, both quality *and* quantity.

So what can we do to encourage communication when we are with our children?

So often parents are telling their children what to do while children are telling their parents their dreams and wishes. Listen to this conversation between a father and his son over tea one evening.

'Dad, I'd really like a skateboard. Ben's got one and skateboards go so fast!'

'Mmm that's very interesting, son. Now eat up. I've got to go out this evening and I want you in bed before the baby-sitter arrives.'

All too often we are so busy with our lives that the children have to fit in. How might Dad have responded?

'They do go fast, don't they and when you are big enough to have one we'll see if we can get one for you. It' s not just the skateboard that goes fast though. It depends on the strength of the rider. You eat up your tea and make yourself strong so that you can ride that skateboard fast one day.'

Sometimes we make the mistake of thinking that communication is the ability to express ourselves. So we talk 'to' our children rather than talking 'with' our children. Communication, when it's working, is not about expressing our thoughts but about drawing out the thoughts of another. Therefore our object in communication with our children must be to understand our child.

How often have we heard or been part of the sort of dinner conversation as above? Our children have very little 'life baggage' that gets in the way of what they are thinking or saying. Therefore what they have to say is very important. How can we learn to listen?

Practical tips.

- Get down to the level of your child. Perhaps kneel or sit when they are talking.
- Look them in the eye. Show them that they have your full attention.
- Don't try and do two things at once. Listen only to your child.

And what will be the end result? Ted Tripp says this, 'Sensitive communication with your children enables them to understand the complexities of life. They learn that life is concerned with both the world of feelings and the world of ideas. It means understanding yourself and others. It means having long term vision as well as short-term goals. It means we become concerned for more than the ,what' or 'what happened' but also about the 'why'.'[2]

So to communicate with your child is to invest long-term in his character. The more you talk with your children, helping them to understand themselves, their temptations, doubts, fears and anxieties, the more you'll prepare them for and give them an understanding of life in the world. And you'll also teach them that their thoughts are of value, that you want to know them, that you want to understand your children better because they matter so much to you.

Imagine this scenario. Your child is putting on his new jumper that your mother in law knitted him for Christmas. You knew when he opened it on Christmas Day that he wasn't really pleased with it but you had asked her to knit him a new jumper and in an error of judgement you had left her to choose the wool and the pattern. Now he is getting ready to go to his friend's house and he is crying. What will you do? If your objective is to let him know your thoughts you might say something like this:

'Look, I know you're not very pleased with that jumper but just put it on and stop looking so miserable. There's nothing the matter with it. Granny spent a lot of time making that for you and you ought to be more grateful. It might not be the style your friends wear but what does that matter? They don't always know what looks best. Now hurry up and get ready or we'll miss the bus.'

On the other hand, if your primary objective was to understand what your child is going through inside, you might have a conversation like this:

'You're fed up about having to wear that jumper, aren't you?'

'Yes'

'You knew as soon as you opened it that you didn't like it, didn't you?'

'Yes, I was really disappointed.'

'But you didn't want to say in case you upset me?'

'No'

'What don't you like about it?'

'It's so uncool. It looks really stupid.'

'I don't know what you mean'

'No-one wears jumpers their Granny knitted. Especially not purple ones.'

'So it's the colour you don't like. And the fact that it's home-made?'

'Yes. All my friends wear fleeces. And the best ones have Nike written on the front. Everyone will think I'm a big girl's blouse wearing this stupid woollen thing. They'll all laugh at me.'

'Everyone will laugh at you. That feels horrible doesn't it?'

'Yes. It makes me feel like I'm really on my own and I don't know where I fit in.'

You have just got in touch with the heart of your child by communicating with him at a deeper level and hearing his inner feelings.

Just recently one of our boys began to complain that he had no friends at school. Initially we responded with 'Of course you have!' and merrily listed the names of all the children in his class we had ever heard him talk about. After all, the teacher had told us that he was popular and always got on well with everyone in the classroom. But he continued to say that he had no friends. This went on for a few days with everyone, including his teacher and his big brother and sister repeatedly telling him that of course he had friends.

Then one day it struck us that whatever the reality

might be, in his little mind he didn't believe he had friends. Sometimes he was alone in the playground and this meant, to him, that he didn't have friends and we needed to take that seriously. And so we changed our response. We began to listen more carefully to what he was saying and to show that we understood how he felt. We made suggestions as to what he might do sometimes to draw his friends to him in the playground and very soon, although he still had times when he was on his own he became his happy self again. Little had changed. His friends were no more his friends now than they had been all along. But because we had listened to him and he had felt understood, he believed we cared, he was then in a stronger position to cope with life in the playground.

We all have three worlds. There is our public world, the part of us that is open for anyone to see. Then there is our personal world, which is open to those close to us. Finally there is our private world which we open up just every now and then to those who we trust.

Children have the same three worlds and from time to time as parents we are invited into that very private world. It may be last thing at night just as your child is settling down to sleep or when you are alone doing a small task together. Often your child will say 'Daddy / Mummy, do you know...' and we find we are invited into their private world. This is a point at which they are about to share something private and personal and our response is crucial. If we tell them not to be so silly or make fun of what they said then they are less likely to open up to us next time.

However if we can be attentive and show we care, however childish the point might be, we are more likely to be invited into their world later on in life when things might not be quite so childish.

Imagine this. A young girl might be talking to her mum or dad one night and in the midst of the conversation she might suddenly say *'Do you think I'm pretty?'* A response such as *'don't be so silly of course you are'* may reassure her to some extent. But how much better to try and get behind the question and discover where it has come from as well as giving the obviously much-needed reassurance. The comment might have come because she was called names at school or because she hears others being told they are pretty but it hasn't been said to her for a while. This is a precious moment and needs careful handling. An appropriate response might be.... *'Yes darling, I do think you're pretty. I think you're beautiful! What makes you ask me that?'*

Remember that communication is the art of expressing in godly ways what is in your heart and of hearing completely and understanding what another thinks or feels.

Allow your children into your world too. Communication is a two-way thing and if we share our heart with our children — let them know what is important to us, what our dreams and visions and hopes are — they will be far more likely to share their hearts with us.

Communication at this deeper level is our aim. Building relationship is the key to that aim. What can we do to build relationship with our children and ensure that they really do feel that we love them?

1 Do things together

If we want a relationship to grow then we will need to commit to it in terms of time. If something means a lot to us, we spend time on it. Our children will know whether they mean a lot to us if we spend time with them. And with children, the best way to spend time together is to do things together — play a game together, go for a walk together, go swimming together, do some gardening together, watch a video together, eat a meal together. Do whatever you like as long as it's together.

Recently Mark was out for the evening and as it was a

Friday, I (Lindsay) suggested to our oldest daughter that she might like to stay up a little later than usual after the younger ones had gone to bed. Her eyes lit up at my suggestion and they became even brighter when I suggested that we might play draughts together. We spent half an hour or so playing our game and chatting and then off she went happily to bed. When I went to bed myself a couple of hours later, on my bed I found a slip of paper on which she had drawn a big heart and inside which she had written in large letters 'I love you'. My guess is that that note came because of the half an hour I had invested earlier in the evening. My time with her had made her feel loved in a way that words alone would probably never have done.

As we spend time with our children we find that very often, good conversation follows, the sort we've talked about above. Making time to do things together creates an environment in which we can talk with our children about important things. And it's worth remembering that our children will probably learn more from talking with their mum and dad than we will ever realise, so it's crucial not to let these opportunities pass us by.

2 Encourage with words

The Bible says in 1 Thessalonians 5:11 'encourage one another and help one another'.

The word *encourage* means 'to instil courage'. In giving a child encouragement we are looking to give him the courage to go further, to enlarge his borders.

We are often so good at praising our work colleagues, our friends' children, neighbours for their garden upkeep or DIY, our friends for their new hairstyle or latest bargain. And yet we are not so good at praising those we love most. Children need to hear words that inspire and encourage them.

As parents we have the power to either discourage or

encourage by what we say to our children. An encouraging word spoken appropriately is often what determines whether a child takes on board the action or attitude we are praising him for.

When our youngest child had a party for her third birthday, there were moments when number three struggled with all the attention his sister was getting! But having settled into it he was able to enjoy seeing her celebrating her birthday. As we tucked both boys into bed, Mark said 'Well done at the party today, chaps. I was proud of the way you joined in and helped Beth to have such a good time.' The grins on their faces said it all. That encouragement really built them up and will no doubt stand them in good stead for the next time they are in a position to be glad for someone else as they celebrate a birthday or something similar.

So speak words of encouragement — 'Thank you for bringing in the milk. That really helps me' when your child has brought the milk in unprompted. Or 'Well done for getting yourself dressed. You've really learnt to do that quickly now' Or 'You've worked really hard at... learning to play football, getting dressed in the morning, leaving your bedroom tidy, picking up your toys... and it's made a real difference.' Words like this that emphasise effort and improvement are such motivators and we have noticed how often such words really help our children to achieve their potential.

Last summer we went to our daughter's sports day and at the end of the afternoon the older girls had the chance to do a long-distance race, right round the field. Jessica had never done anything like this and we wondered how she would fare! Mark decided he would run round with her on the inside of the track so as to encourage her every step of the way. She got off to a good start and was near the front but as time went on she began to flag. At this point Mark shouted as loud as he could 'Come on Jessica! You can do it! Don't give up now! Keep going!' at which we visibly saw her muster up all the strength she could and surge forwards once again. She didn't win but she was amongst the first to finish and was delighted with herself. Later that evening we found a note on our pillow addressed to her Daddy which read 'I love you, Daddy, I would never have come 6th in the marathon if you didn't cheer me on and do it with me. Thank you for coming to sports day and encouraging me.'

Words don't have to be spoken, they can be written too. We often write a note and pop it in the children's lunch box or leave it amongst their work when we've been to parents' evening or simply on their pillow. Sometimes these written words are even more precious because they can be kept and looked at again another day.

Remember too... allow your children the freedom to fail.

For any child to be told that they are a failure is so disheartening. Saying *'Come on, you are 6 years old now, you should be able to tie your own laces'* as a parent takes over and ties the laces up for the child, is very different from saying, *'You try really hard to tie your laces these days. Well done. Would you like me to help you learn so that you can do them on your own?'*

If our children are afraid of failing and of looking fool-

ish they may well hold back rather than stretching themselves to their full potential. They need to know that as long as they have tried their best, failure is fine and that we will always stand by them. Last summer on the way home from our sons' sports day, the younger of the two was gaily reminding us that he had won 2 medals and wasn't it a shame that his brother hadn't won any. Wanting to find a way of encouraging both of them at once I said to them, "I am very pleased with both of you. You have both done your best today and that is what counts. The most important thing is always to try your best." Our older boy's face was a picture. He beamed and was as happy as anything as he skipped home wearing the medal his mum had been determined to win in the Mothers Race. So that he wouldn't be without one!

An encouraging parent looks for effort rather than success and so in all our parenting we do well always to look for improvement and seek to encourage and inspire our children in every way possible.

3 Give plenty of physical hugs

Don't forget to give your children plenty of hugs. Studies have shown that many parents only touch their children when it is necessary such as when they are dressing them or putting them in the car or taking them up to bed. It seems that lots of parents don't appreciate how much their children need to be touched and what an effective way this is of making their children feel loved.

As parents, we need to develop a relationship with our children that is not just verbal but is also physical. This will mean hugging our children when we want to congratulate them as well as hugging them when they are hurting.

To deprive our children of physical hugs now might mean that they will have difficulty hugging us when they leave home and yet it might well be the very thing they still need. Children of all ages and both sexes need physical expression of love. A son needs his father's loving touch as well as his mother's and a daughter needs plenty of physical affection from her mother as well as from her father.

Author Paul Planet says this:

> 'Hugging is very healthy. It helps the body's immune system. It keeps you healthier. It cures depression and reduces stress. It induces sleep. It is invigorating. It is rejuvenating. It has no unpleasant side effects. Hugging is nothing less than a miracle drug. Hugging is all natural. It is organic and naturally sweet. It contains no pesticides, preservatives or artificial ingredients and is 100% wholesome.
>
> Hugging is practically perfect. There are no moveable parts, no batteries to wear out, no periodic check-ups, no monthly payments, no insurance requirements. It offers no energy consumption and returns a high-energy yield while being inflation-proof, non-fattening, theft-proof, non-taxable, non-polluting and fully-returnable.'[3]

Be the example of relationship with your wife/husband

In the previous chapter we were reminded of how God made man and woman to be together and that they were complete without children. As we demonstrate our love for one another in front of the children we create an environment where our children feel safe and where they see long term committed love demonstrated. This is especially true in the area of physical touch. We are role models for our children. They will be watching the way we practice physical touch. And it's a wonderful thing to see our children using physical touch as they relate to one another and to family and friends. Nothing could be healthier.

Remember: if children *feel* genuinely loved by their parents, they will be more responsive to parental guidance in all areas of their lives.

4 Keep your promises

I know that this is rather stating the obvious but to build trust and communication we have to be trustworthy. 'I'll play with you later' rolls all too easily off the tongue, in order to solve an immediate situation. We may forget to play but our children won't forget and if we cannot be trustworthy and people of our word then why should they be?

Our memories are all too short but our children's are not. Children remember more than we realise and they'll remember if we let them down.

5 Tell your children regularly that you love them

All children need to be told in words that Mum and Dad love them. For some people, especially if it was never said to them as children, this may not come easily but it is worth persevering and practising at every opportunity.

In our family we not only say the words verbally, we often write them down and also use signing to get our message across. The children love this 'secret' way of communicating our love, and it's especially fun in a crowded place such as a school concert or when you're saying goodbye at the school gate and you don't want your child to lose face with his friends.

And finally... a word to the dads...

A recent article in The Times (28/1/99) said this, 'Fathers who devote time to their sons — even as little as five minutes a day — are giving them a far greater chance to grow up as confident adults, a parenting research project has found.' It went on, 'Boys who feel that their fathers devote time especially to them and talk about their worries, school work and social lives almost all emerge as motivated and optimistic young men full of confidence and hope'. **Building boys is better than mending men.**

The Bible says that fathers have a special responsibility in a family. They are to give a lead. Dad is the head of the home and as such should set the example in many things. All too often today dads are absent from the home for much of the time and so find it difficult to fulfil their God given duty to their wife and children.

We dads need to remember that the way we respond to our God-given responsibility in the family will determine whether or not our children grow up in a healthy family, confident and secure in themselves.

When our children are young we mums and dads are largely in control of all they do. God made it this way because our children have been entrusted to us and we, through our love and care, will look after them. As they grow older though, our *control* diminishes as they begin to make their own decisions and choices and we hope that in its place comes our *influence* to guide them in how they live their lives.

But our influence will only be as great as the effort we have put into making strong relationships. Our aim must be to build a relationship that will stand the test of time. It's as we spend time with our children now, building a relationship of trust, that we are laying the foundations for a life of unity in the family.

BIBLE VERSES USED IN THIS CHAPTER

1 Thessalonians 5:11

Acknowledgements

1 Rob Parsons, *The Sixty Minute Father,* Hodder and Stoughton,
2 Tedd Tripp, *Shepherding a Child's Heart,* Shepherd Press New York,
3 Paul Planet, *Let's Hug, Once upon a Planet,* 1981, Bay Side, New York

Recommended reading for this chapter

The Five Love Languages for Children by Gary Chapman & Ross Campbell, MD, Northfield Publishing, Chicago
The Sixty Minute Father, Rob Parsons, Hodder & Stoughton

Questions for discussion groups

1 How good are you at hearing what your children or even other people are saying? How far have you already sought to encourage your child to express himself?

2 Do you think there is a cost involved in seeking to communicate with our children in the ways we've

discussed in this chapter?35

3 Can you share your own ideas about how you have spent time with your children and invested in relationship-building?

4 It's so often easier to criticise than to encourage. What changes might you have to make if you were to work on encouraging your child?

Application points...

1 Begin to work on listening and communicating in the way suggested and note whether your child responds differently.

2 Pick three practical points that you feel you can put into practice this week in your family life and again note the response.

3 Review your example as a couple in the way you relate and listen to each other. Talk together about the example you are setting for your children.

4

PULLING THEIR STRINGS — THE FAMILY

We well remember the day our daughter was born, being so over-awed by this tiny baby lying in the little cot in the hospital. She was absolutely beautiful, not a blemish on her. She looked absolutely perfect. Within a very short time though, we began to realise what a responsibility it was to be caring for this little thing. The way we treated her would ultimately have quite an effect on how she turned out. We began to realise that even at only a few days old, she could demand our attention constantly. And we could either rush to pick her up immediately, or we could begin to teach her that she is not the centre of everything and that there are times when we need time to ourselves or with each other, and she needs to sleep because that is the best thing for her.

As parents we quickly become aware that children are like sponges: they absorb what they are exposed to incredibly easily and from day one, our children are being shaped and moulded by life's circumstances and by the influences around them. All the issues of family life have a profound impact on the people our children will eventually become.

Every child will be subject to certain shaping influences, events and circumstances in the developmental years, which prove to be catalysts for making him the person he is. The Bible makes it very clear that our early childhood experience has life-long implications for every individual. Some of the major passages in the Bible that deal with family life give guidance on how children should be treated and brought up (e.g. Deuteronomy 6; Ephesians 6; and Colossians 3). Also much has been written, both Christian and secular, about the bearing that our foundational years of childhood have on us as a whole.

But the shaping is not automatic. Just as important as the effect of these events and circumstances is the way the child responds to them. It is this response that will determine the effect these influences ultimately have upon him.

There are two things which determine the kind of people our children will become. The first is their life experience. What is life like for this child? In what environment is he being brought up? Are both parents around? The second is how he interacts with that experience. Our children react and respond to their circumstances, and our job as parents is to know where our children need guidance and structure to help them respond appropriately so that they are not blown hither and thither by every wind which comes in their direction.

In these next two chapters we are going to focus on some of the positive and negative influences which our children are under in today's world and the effect that those influences have. We are going to be looking at what steps we can take as wise parents to keep those influences in check. In this chapter we look at the role of the family and the impact it has on our children. In the next chapter we'll look at other influences and their effect on our children and then finally at our children's relationship with God and the important part that plays in determining how they respond to all these other things.

The Family

When our children are very young the family is one of the major influences on them. As they grow older, and start to make friends of their own there is a tendency for this influence to diminish and what other people say becomes increasingly important. If we are wise, we will take time to stand back and take a look at our family life, the impact it is having on our children and decide whether there are things we need to do to strengthen it so that it can remain a positive influence which will help to shape our children's future life and values, even when they hit the teenage years and beyond.

There are many aspects of family life that have a bearing on who our children become. Here are some of them:

Family Structure

The structure of the family in a child's particular situation is one of the most obvious factors that will affect him. He will be affected by such things as whether or not he is part of a traditional nuclear family; whether he lives with one or both parents and whether they are available or alternatively, physically or emotionally absent. Do grandparents live nearby and play an active part in family life or do they live at a distance? Is your child an only child or does he have siblings? Are your children close in age, ability and personality? Is there a step-parent in the home or step brothers and sisters?

Family Roles

Within any family the roles played by each member will vary. Some fathers are preoccupied and unavailable, others are very much involved in every aspect of family life. In some families the mother takes complete responsibility for the child care, in others it is the father who is chiefly responsible for the practical day-to-day running of the family.

Children, too, have differing roles. Much is expected of some children in the home and almost nothing is expected of others. Within our families we need to assess what our roles are. It is a shaping factor in the lives of our children. Will they see Dad doing the washing-up and sweeping the kitchen floor or is it just Mum? What model are we showing to our children through our roles? I (Mark) grew up in a family where I was encouraged to do some of my own ironing, I was given the freedom to cook meals for myself and it was generally expected that I help around the house. This has helped me in adult life. I find it a natural thing to pick up the iron or vacuum the house and in so doing I hope that I am modelling team work to my children so that they will do the same in their family when they eventually marry and have children of their own.

Family Conflict

The way problems are approached varies enormously from family to family and cannot fail to have a huge bearing on the children's ability to face life's difficulties. Does the family know how to talk through problems in order to resolve them? Are problems swept under the carpet in order to keep the peace? The Bible says in Proverbs 12:15,16 'The way of a fool seems right to him, but a wise man listens to advice. A fool shows his annoyance at once, but a prudent man overlooks an insult.' If conflict is dealt with wisely and sensitively, a child will learn that problems are better resolved than ignored. In this way the influence of the home helps the children to think things through carefully and be wise in their decisions.

Family Failure

We touched on this in chapter 3 where we said that if a child is free to fail without being criticised or laughed at he will grow in confidence, knowing that even if he does make a mistake it is not the end of the world. If parents can see failed attempts as praiseworthy efforts, always encouraging their children, this will be a very positive shaping influence in his life.

Family History

Every family has a history and each one is different. There are births, deaths, marriages, divorces, house moves, job moves, financial concerns, sickness, accidents and so on. Some families have lived in the neighbourhood for generations and the children have grown up with their friends and family around them, whilst others have continually moved around and the children have had to make new friends and cope with new situations on a regular basis. Again, all of these considerations will have a profound effect on the lives of our children.

Family Values

Every family has values of some sort, that is developed attitudes, ideas and beliefs which affect the way we operate. What is important to the parents? What is worth a fuss and what passes without notice? Are people more important than things? Do parents get more stressed over a hole in a school jumper or a fight between school friends? What philosophies and ideas does the child hear? What are the spoken and unspoken rules of family life? Where does God fit into family life? Is life organised around knowing and loving God or not? What is important in the home?

We are going on to look at this in more detail in another chapter. However it is worth saying here that if we are to share our values with our children then we have to start while they are young.

Clearly, as parents we must be concerned with providing the most stable influences for our children. Some of the things we have mentioned above are already established (such as family history and family structure) and so in a sense there is nothing we can do to change their effect on our children. But others are very much open to change and we will do well to take an honest look at our families and ask ourselves a few questions. Is ours a family where our children are free to fail in the knowledge that they will always be loved unconditionally? Are we, as a family, offering our children a secure place in which to learn to discuss issues and resolve problems openly and sensibly? Are we happy with the example we set as parents in terms of the roles we have in the home?

It is never an indication of failure to see a need to make changes in family life. And it is never too late. With God's help and our own motivation we can always improve things. Now is the time to be proactive in our families and change things for the better if we need to.

We've begun, then, to look at how our families help to shape the lives of our children in a positive way. Now we are going to focus on something further that we believe to be of great importance in determining whether our children respond to all our positive shaping and input and whether they ultimately hold on to what we have taught them when other influences in their lives get stronger.

Family Identity

Peer pressure is something that all of us are very aware of and we perhaps think that there is nothing that we can do to lessen its influence. We believe however that if we have a strong family identity then peer pressure is diminished. If family identity is strong, if our children feel involved in and proud to belong to their family, they are far more likely to hold to its values and principles. On the other hand, children who feel uninvolved in their family and have little sense of belonging are more likely to look outside the family for a sense of identity and a set of values.

Of course, there are exceptions, but having worked with groups of young people in the course of our ministry, it has been evident to us that those who come from families who appear to be a strong unit cope so much better in the face of temptation by friends. To help our children avoid getting involved in activities that will lead them into trouble we can start by working at our family identity. We've noticed others, too, who seem to have little time or affection for their families who very willingly follow the crowd. There is great security in belonging to a group and where family ties are weak, young people need to find that security with friends. How, then, can we build a strong family identity?

Be a team

Being a team encourages a family to be interdependent. All too often parents today encourage their children to be independent too soon. This can very quickly lead to a lack of family identity. If we give our children too much freedom to do their own thing too soon, they will have generally tried most things by the time they are 17 and then go onto try the things we would rather they didn't get involved in just to find the next thrill!

Interdependence encourages family unity and identity. It's amazing what strength and resources we can find within us if we encourage and are encouraged by those we are working with. Teams, when they work together can achieve a great deal.

I believe that those of us who are dads have a special role here and should give the lead in being a team. We need to encourage everyone and always let it be known that we think our family is great to be part of, that everyone is important and that we should be looking out for each other.

I am always encouraging my team. 'Come on, you guys'; 'How are we doing, team?'; 'Come on team!' are words that often come from my lips. The more we can build a sense of team spirit, the more we can build a family that works and plays together, the stronger our family identity will be.

Being a team means supporting and encouraging the members. When we watched our daughter at school taking part in her sports day, I noticed how the girls ran not for themselves as much as for their parents. It was the cheering from the mums and dads that made the difference. I also noticed those girls whose parents hadn't been able to be there and how they were looking for support from their class mates.

I've now noticed that my children often say to each other, 'we're the Melluish team'. They are proud to be a team and, though we never take it for granted, we pray that that will always be the case.

Family Time

One activity that we and many others have found helpful in building strong foundations and relationships in family life is what we call Family Time. In fact we think it is so important, we have given this book that very title!

In chapter 2 we looked at making our marriage the primary relationship in a family and saw how the children extend the family but don't complete it. Family Time is simply putting this into action. It is an activity that allows us to live out what we believe about the family.

Family Time is simply time put by first for Mum and Dad to have time alone together or with God and then time for the children to join in for their time to share too. So how does this work? In our family, because I work from home, Lindsay and I often find some time together at about 5.30 p.m. This is when the children are home from school and are full of life! We often put the kettle on and make a pot of tea and then tell the children that Mum and Dad are going to have some time on their own. During this time the children are encouraged to 'find something to do'. This might be finishing homework or getting a game out. We then sit down with our tea and have time for a chat about the day's events. This allows us to catch up with each other and to share about the day. As we've said, we feel that it is important to do this with the children around so that they can see the value and importance of Mum and Dad spending time together. Then once we have had 10 minutes to ourselves the children come and talk about their day.

Family Time gives every member of the family time to talk and time to listen. It allows members of the family to share their dreams and visions. It provides an opportunity to share hurts and feelings. It lets every member of the family know that what they say is important as well as teaching listening and talking skills. Through Family Time we help our children to express what is on their hearts and we can encourage them to be thoughtful of others.

Friends of ours have Family Time first thing in the morning because of the demands of work. This means that they find time first thing in the morning to talk together as a couple and then invite the children to join them on the bed for sharing. There is no right or wrong time or place or way to have Family Time. What matters is that it works for *your* family.

To have Family Time now helps us as parents to equip our children as they get older for all walks of life. It will provide a place where children can ask about all sorts of things and because we have been talking and listening on a regular basis we will have that safe place in which to talk naturally about such things.

It also means that we can drip feed information. We as parents are to be responsible for teaching our children about subjects such as sex and the big question is 'When is the right time?' The truth is of course that we must not be pressured by what the papers say or what our friends say because it will be different for everyone. Little by little helps so that our children know enough but not too much. The story goes of one parent who felt that the time was right when her son came and asked where he had come from. Mum then went into great detail about the male and female bodies and described what Mum

and Dad did to express love and how this resulted in a baby. After about 20 minutes the son looked at his mother and said, 'Well that's funny, because Jonny says he came from Cornwall'[1]

The point is we are to give as much information as seems appropriate at the time, ensuring we don't overload or confuse our children. Family Time is a regular 'slot' for doing just that!

Of course Family Time won't be the only time we talk with our children! Often children talk when they want to and maybe they won't feel like it at Family Time. We need to be ready to talk at other times too! But we have found that the children love having this special slot for them and generally the response is good!

Family Jobs

Children who are waited on by their parents may never learn to take some of the responsibility of running the home. We all laugh at the Andy Capp image of men. Andy Cap is a beer-drinking layabout who is waited on hand and foot by his long-suffering wife, but for a few, this can be real life. Helping around the home doesn't need to be seen as a chore. Our children all have jobs and we make them times of communication or learning.

Our four year old son has the job of setting the table for tea each day. Lindsay is generally in the kitchen making tea at the same time and so this has become a time for them to talk while they are working together for the rest of the family.

Our other son sets the table for breakfast so he is encouraged to get dressed quickly in order to help all of us have a good start to the day. One daughter clears the table after each meal and feeds the cats which she enjoys doing. Her sister tidies her toys away each morning after she has been playing in her room so that it is ready for the next day.

We have found that this creates a greater sense of family unity. And we shouldn't be fooled into believing that our children are too young to have a job! So often we've heard parents say, 'Oh I can't expect my children to do jobs yet. They are too young and they might not do them properly.' Children will surely only learn if they are allowed to have a go, and in the safety of the home where we can stand by to help and guide them. Below is a list of jobs that your children might do to help around the home. There will be many others that you can think of that relate to your family. You might like to consider which jobs your children would be up to doing already and which ones they might do fairly soon.

Set the table for a meal
Feed pets
Make drinks
Make beds in the morning
Help with cleaning
Tidy garden of toys
Pick up litter in garden
Make cups of tea or coffee
Clear up their toys after use
Put dirty clothes in the wash basket
Clean windows
Wash car
Help with washing up
Help with ironing
Help with the gardening
Cook a meal

Giving our children jobs to do builds a sense of responsibility. As we trust them to wash up or we trust them to feed the pets we encourage them to do their bit in the family. We believe too, as we've said before, that those jobs which affect the whole family such as laying the table are very good for encouraging a sense of team spirit and a willingness later in life to muck in where help is needed.

In all of this we need to be very wise. Too much responsibility too early could be overwhelming, but too little could leave them believing that you don't trust them. It is also very important to understand that by giving our children responsibility we are not washing our hands of our role and responsibility as parents. It is us sharing our responsibility with them. This means that we are always checking to see how they are getting on with their jobs rather then getting cross when things don't happen as they should.

Family Quote Book

All children, and adults too, come out with hilarious and sometimes embarrassing quotes that cause many a laugh. Another way of building this sense of being a team is to have a family quote book. In it write down some of the funnier family quotes. And as they get older they can write in it too. Here are three funny moments our family remembers well!

Our two year old, daughter was recently looking longingly at a Barbie doll during our staff lunch. We didn't pay much attention until suddenly she pointed to Barbie's bosoms and announced to everyone 'I'd like some of these.' It was one of those golden moments that we would have loved to keep on video.

I was driving our two boys to school recently and because our son was a little rusty on his recorder homework Lindsay asked if I would listen to him in the car. This I did with pleasure and he was doing very well playing through Old MacDonald had a farm, until about half way through when he suddenly stopped and looked out of the car window. 'What are you doing son' I asked, 'You're only half way through the piece'. 'No daddy, I'm meant to stop here' came the reply, "There's a rest in the music!'

Some time after our son had finished with nappies, he noticed that some boys didn't sit down when they went to the toilet. This bothered him slightly probably because it made him feel a little babyish, but we encouraged him to continue sitting down for a while until he grew bigger. He took to taking note of how people went about going to the toilet and one day Grandpa came to stay and at the tea table our son suddenly turned to him and said, 'Grandpa, do you stand up to do your wees?'

In our family we often refer back to the things people have said in the past and the way in which they said it. This creates a family history as well as helping to build a very real sense of belonging.

Family Photos

Having photos around the home is another great way of recording family history and giving the family a sense of identity. Lindsay has taken to creating a collage at the end of the year which includes photographs of all the important events — birthdays, Christmas, weddings and so on — that have taken place during the year. We have one for each year that our children have been alive, on the wall at home. So a quick look around our kitchen will give you a brief family history over the last nine years.

This is great for the children. Children have such a limited concept of time and yet a few photos on the wall remind them that they were small once. It will allow them to look back at holidays and special moments. And they love to look and remind themselves of what cake they had when they were 2, 3, 4, 5 and so on. It helps keep in focus the fact that we are a family and that we do things together.

Don't forget to have some photos up of Mum and Dad without the children too, before the children came along or even since. It's good for everyone to see those types of photo too.

Family Traditions

Do you rip open your presents at 4:30 am or are you a 'We'll wait until after lunch' family on Christmas day? It's these sorts of things that build family traditions. There is no right or wrong way. There is simply a family way. When we first got married we soon discovered on our first Christmas that we had different family traditions. Lindsay's family would do things one way and my family did it another. We choose to do it our way and it has become our tradition.

It's not just at Christmas, though. We always visit a roadside restaurant on our way on holiday. It's something we started and now our children look forward to it. They know that we are going to stop for breakfast or dinner depending on what time of day we are travelling. It's become a family tradition.

Last week it was our son's birthday and he was, naturally, very excited. He came into our bedroom the day before and snuggled up to us and said, 'Tomorrow is the day when I will come in and sit between you both and the others will be down the other end of the bed and I'll open my presents, won't I?' Neither of us had realised how the precise detail of that family ritual was so important in his little life.

Family traditions are simply another way of saying 'this is us and this is the way we do things together.'

Be Together

'Families who spend significant amounts of time together as a unit are also more likely to turn out confident children', a parenting research project called Tomorrow's Men, supported by Oxford University, has found. It is of course no surprise to many of us, but it is sadly something that is generally a low priority in many families today.

There are times when life can be so busy with after-school activities, sports clubs, recorder lessons, piano lessons, football coaching, Cubs, Brownies and the many other things that crop up daily. It is therefore important that we are creative in our family activities as well.

Make meal times a must. Eating together builds a sense of belonging. Sometimes eating separately is necessary for convenience but it's important to remember that meal times can be a great time to talk, catch up on news and be doing an activity together. We are aware that the fact that I work from home makes it easy for us to eat together as a family. It is much more difficult in families where work commitments make it impossible to have a family meal every day. If that's the case, make Sunday lunch special, or Friday evening. Whatever fits into your family schedule.

Do things together. Recently I spent a few hours in the garden and made the most of the time by asking our eldest son to help me. As we worked we talked about our family and how we were making the garden special for everyone to use. It also gave us an opportunity to laugh together, when I fell out of a tree and onto a pile of weeds! Here are some suggestions for activities to do together:

- Cycle rides
- Shopping
- Have a family Pizza night with a good video

- Go for walks together
- Eat meals together as often as possible
- Sleep in the tent together in the garden
- Sit in church together
- Eat ice creams together
- Do the gardening together

It doesn't matter what you do as long as you all enjoy it and you do it together.

Make family holidays a priority. So often we hear of families who rarely go on holiday together. We believe that holidays are a must. And we're not talking about expensive trips abroad to sunny places, necessarily. Camping holidays are cheap and just as fun. The important thing is to get away together, away from the busyness, and have time doing fun things together and investing in family memories.

All these activities and any others you can think of become important highlights in the lives of our families. They help to show our commitment to the family and to

build trust. We often say to our children 'come on, we are the Melluish's and we do it this way' and such a simple statement gives us a sense of being a team, of being together and having common aims. Our children will remember these good times. And they create precious memories for everyone to look back on.

It might be worth asking ourselves these questions...

1. Are we cultivating a sense of team spirit within our family or is independence valued more than interdependence?
2. Is our family one that our children are proud to belong to? Are we giving them good reason to be proud?
3. Do our children feel involved in our family?

The family is a crucial factor in determining who our children become and we have an opportunity to invest time and energy now that will reap many rewards later in life. It's always easier to build something from scratch rather than trying to repair something that is already built. Let's build strong families for our children to grow up in and pray that they in turn will do the same for their children.

BIBLE REFERENCES USED IN THIS CHAPTER

Deuteronomy 6
Ephesians 6
Colossians 3
Proverbs 12:15,16

Acknowledgements

1 An illustration adapted from: Steve Chalke, *How to succeed as a parent*, Hodder & Stoughton 1997

Questions for discussion groups

1 Family circumstances play an important role in children's lives. Talk, if you can, about what you have noticed in families around you in terms of the effect of family set-up on the children.

2 Can you share some of your own personal childhood experiences, considering such things as family conflict, family failure and role models?. Are you aware of things you grew up with that have had a positive or negative effect on you?

3 Did you grow up in a family with a strong identity? If so, what made it strong?

4 What about our families now? Can we see strong identities developing or are there steps we need to take to strengthen them?

Application points...

1 Consider the structure of your family and what effect it might have on your child or children. Are there things that you would like to change?

2 Consider steps you might take to strengthen the identity of your family.

3 Try having Family Time and note the results.

5

WHO ELSE IS INFLUENCING OUR CHILDREN?

How we all love to see the intense pleasure on a child's face when we suggest doing something exciting with them. 'Let's go for a ride on our bikes in the park' or 'Let's sit and read a story together' are words that children love to hear from their parents.

However, although it is generally the main influence in our children's lives, the family can seem to become one of the least. As our children grow older and begin to have freedom to be a bit more independent, outside influences become stronger and they are going to be faced not only with positive ideas and activities but negative ones as well. We as parents need to be on the alert to these influences, making sure we try and prepare our children for this and equip them to make decisions based on what is right and good.

At as young as 7 years old or even earlier, our children are being affected by different opinions on all sorts of subjects: sex, drugs, music, the environment, money, fashion, religion, war, animal rights, homosexuality, careers, food, art, transport, race, gender, language, sport... and so on. Often this is just other people expressing their opinions. But sometimes it is a deliberate attempt to persuade our children to hold the same beliefs or attitude as them. Sometimes financial gain is the motive, as in the case of the advertising. Sometimes it is people looking to justify what they are getting into by pressurising their friends to do the same. Smoking, sex, drugs and drinking are cases in point. Let's take a closer look at some of the influences our children are under outside the family.

The television

Statistics tell us that the average father spends three minutes a day in 'quality' conversation with his children and the average mother, five and a half minutes. On the other hand, the average child spends three hours a day watching television. Some children have televisions in their bedrooms and many sitting-rooms are arranged around the television and meals are always eaten in front of the television. If this is the case, most of the children's values and morals will be shaped by what they see on television.

Of course, television is part of our culture and much about it is good. But we do need to be careful what our children watch. The Bible says, 'Whatever is true, noble, right, pure, whatever is lovely, admirable... think about

such things.' Does what our children watch fit into this category? Some of the very popular children's cartoon films, for example, are frightening with a very real evil presence. There are so many lovely things in this world, and how much better to fill our children's minds with good things. We have to be selective and not just assume that because it's on children's television it is either helpful or healthy to watch.

We use a video recorder to record programmes that we know our children would enjoy so that the programme is then available to us when we are ready to watch it.

Christian videos are also available for hire or purchase.

At the time of writing this, a letter in the Times (Feb 11th 1999) expressed just the kind of thing we are hoping to communicate. It refers to comments made about 'Blue Peter' a children's programme that has stood the test of time and is watched by millions of children every week.

From Mrs S Denniston

Sir, We are informed that Stuart Miles, the presenter of Blue Peter, is leaving the programme as it affords too 'twee' and 'comfort blanket' an approach to life (report Feb 8th later editions).

Perhaps Mr Miles has grown up. For too many children, however, childhood is increasingly short and 'hard hitting'. Is it a bad thing that a programme aimed at children should not set out to 'shock or offend'? That the programme makers at Blue Peter aim to inform and educate within the realm of childhood should be applauded. It is a rare thing as we force our children towards an ever younger understanding of an adult world.

Let us be brave. Let us err on the side of caution with our children.

The school

Often we have little control over who will teach our children when they are at school and inevitably their teachers' attitudes will be passed onto our children. However school life is so influential in the lives of our children that we believe it should be a place where we become involved if we possibly can. This might be through offering classroom help or by being on a parent committee or governing body.

We also need to be aware of what material is being used in our schools. So for example, find out what books are they reading — so often young children come home with a reading book about witches and ghosts. If this is the case, we can perhaps suggest others and offer to help the school review what material is available. Recently our daughter was required to read a book which she said she found frightening. We encouraged her to explain this to the teacher who supported her in finding another book. So often it just takes a quiet word in a teacher's ear for things to change.

Schools are there to help our children to learn and the majority of teachers are very open to help and suggestions as long as we don't take over. They have a job to do and they do it in a professional and efficient way. Lets ensure that we work with the teachers who have care of our children so that we can support them as well as have them support us and our children.

Friends

After their family, our children's friends will have the greatest influence on them. Some of these friends will influence positively and some negatively. We need to encourage our children to choose their friends wisely and sometimes we would do well to discourage a friendship if it is having a negative effect on our children.

This is not to say that we would want the children to be unfriendly or standoffish with certain people. We want them to show kindness to everyone they know and would welcome any friend they brought home. However if we noticed that a particular friendship was having a bad influence on our child we might actively encourage them to be in touch with some of their friends who encourage them in life. We are told in Proverbs 13:20: 'He who walks with the wise grows wise, but a companion of fools suffers harm' and Paul says in 1 Corinthians 15:33, 'bad company corrupts good character.' We can choose friends for our children when they are very young and after this we have to gently educate them to be wise about their friendships.

Our sons come home singing all sorts of songs about different football teams and talking about a whole variety of games and television characters that we know they know nothing about. This is simply peer pressure and it starts when they are very young. We therefore encourage friendships with those who obviously come from like-minded families and therefore reinforce the values we hold. Our daughter developed a friendship with a school friend very early on in her school life and it was a friendship that she and we enjoyed. We have therefore encouraged her in this friendship because we feel it is helpful to her in every way and over the past 5 years these two have become 'best' friends.

Other adults

Apart from school teachers there are other adults who also influence our children — friends' parents, child-minders, teachers of outside activities like ballet or football, church children's group leaders and so on. We need to keep an eye on these relationships and encourage those relationships with adults whose values we respect and want passed on to our children.

We have a youth minister in our church who is responsible for the young people's work from age 7 — 18. Our children already think he is one of the greatest. They talk about him at the tea table and will often comment on what he has said. He is someone who in the lives of our own and lots of other people's children will have a positive effect and so we make every effort to support all that he does. This once meant coming home from holiday a day early so that the children could be at a party he was holding.

There are so many influences. Look at this list and note down how many hours each week your children spend with this person or doing that activity. Then ask yourself how helpful or otherwise that is. Try to be as specific as possible.

TV & Video	Books, magazines and comics
Friends	Family
Other adults	Church, youth and children's groups
Clubs	Parents
School	Other

Perhaps it is also worth asking the following questions...

Who do you think has the greatest influence on your

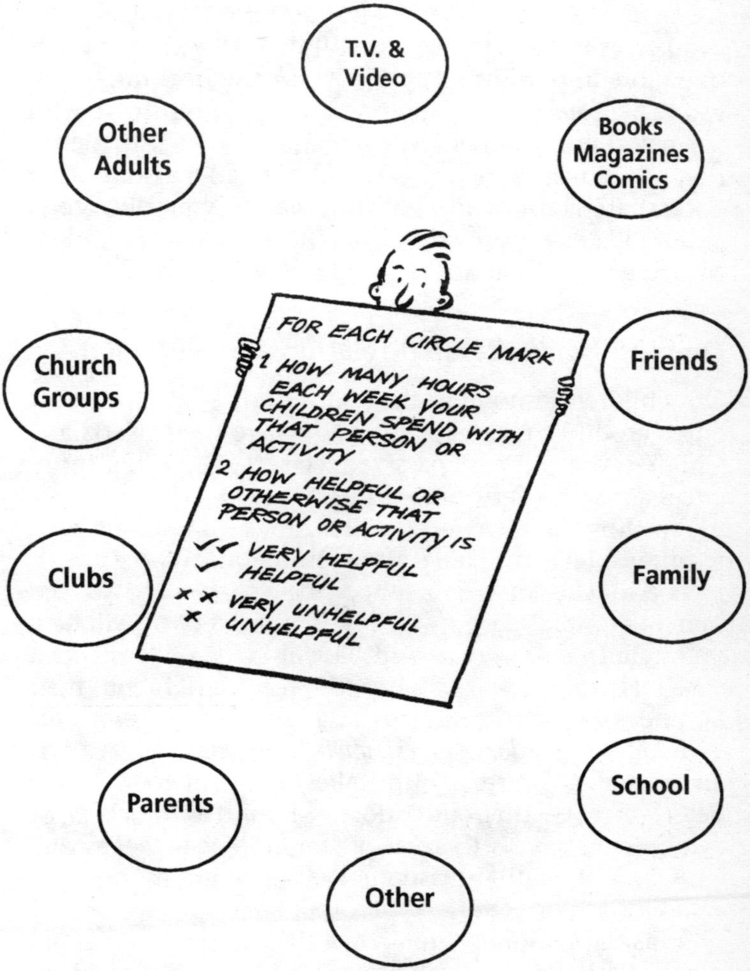
T.V. & Video
Other Adults
Books Magazines Comics
FOR EACH CIRCLE MARK
1 HOW MANY HOURS EACH WEEK YOUR CHILDREN SPEND WITH THAT PERSON OR ACTIVITY
2 HOW HELPFUL OR OTHERWISE THAT PERSON OR ACTIVITY IS
✓✓ VERY HELPFUL
✓ HELPFUL
× × VERY UNHELPFUL
× UNHELPFUL
Church Groups
Friends
Clubs
Family
Parents
School
Other

children? Are you happy about this influence? Does anything need changing? How many other people are bringing up your children?

We do well, then, to pay great attention to all of these influences in the lives of our children. However, there is one more important thing to say. We might think that if we can protect our children, always be positive with them and provide them with the best possible experience then they will turn out OK. But we can't assume that good shaping influences will automatically produce good children. If we do, we are forgetting that our children themselves have an active part to play in all of this.

Our children's personal relationship with God

Our children respond to their surroundings, to the influences around them, according to where their hearts are. Children are not just passive receivers of outside influences. They are active responders.

Proverbs 9:7–10 contrasts the mocker's and the wise man's response to rebuke and instruction. 'Whoever corrects a mocker invites insult; whoever rebukes a wicked man incurs abuse. Do not rebuke a mocker or he will hate you; rebuke a wise man and he will love you. Instruct a wise man and he will be wiser still; teach a righteous man and he will add to his learning. *The fear of the Lord is the beginning of wisdom, and knowledge of the Holy One is understanding.*' Verse 10 (in italics) helps us to see what determines whether our children respond as 'mockers' or as 'wise men'. It is the fear of the Lord that makes one wise and it is that wisdom that determines how he responds to correction.

So as our children interact with their childhood experience, their response will be affected by their perception of God. They are either growing in an understanding of who God is, or they are unaware of what it means to love and be loved by him.

Part of our task as parents is to help our children to worship and honour God in their lives. Of course we want to provide the best possible shaping influences for our children, making sure the structure of our home provides the stability and security that they need. Of course we want the quality of relationships in our home to reflect the grace of God and the forgiveness for failure that God's character demonstrates. Of course we want to use appropriate discipline so that our home is not chaotic but rather well-structured. Of course we want to provide a healthy, constructive atmosphere for our children. But this is not the whole story. Our children's response to God in all of this, our children's own relationship with God is what will determine their response to life. We need to be directing our children towards knowing, serving and honouring God.

How can we do that?

Pray for them regularly that they will develop their own relationship with God. We started praying for our children before they were conceived and have not stopped praying since. Like all families we have had our share of knocks and scrapes and have twice had to call 999 for one of our children. So praying for them does not necessarily mean that they will be accident free and live long healthy lives. However it does mean that there will always be a channel open between their lives and God.

As our children have grown we have enjoyed seeing some of our prayers answered. I'm sure that we are not the only parents that pray as we see our children off to school for the first time, or as they share about being alone in the playground with 'no friends'. We have always taken prayer to be the starting point at all times with our children.

Start praying before they are even conceived. I well remember lying in bed talking about when we might start a family and Lindsay saying that the chances were that our baby's future husband or wife might just be being conceived now or may already be alive. We started praying there and then for the future partners of our children.

Prayer for the unborn child or even the child yet to be conceived is important. When a baby girl is born she has within her all the eggs that will later in life produce some children, God willing. So when Lindsay and I prayed about conceiving we knew that within Lindsay was the beginning of life itself and that one of those eggs would become our first child.

We have also had the privilege of praying for couples who have had trouble conceiving. Lindsay and I have our own story to tell of how we continued having children after the birth of our first child. Like many other couples, we planned a two year gap between the births of our children. However after trying to conceive our second child for quite a while with nothing happening, we were advised to have some tests. It became evident that Lindsay's fallopian tubes had become blocked and so no eggs were able to pass down them. At the thought of having no more children we wept, prayed, felt angry, let down and went through every other emotion you can think of.

A short while after receiving our bad news, a friend turned up on the doorstep to say that he had been on holiday in Greece where he had had a dream about us and felt that we were in some sort of trouble. Lindsay and I explained about our pain of not having more children and about the cost of having an operation to open up tubes which we couldn't afford. Barry then said that God can easily open up tubes and prayed for us. He also counselled that we seek out every bit of medical help we could because God often uses our doctors. This we did as well as taking a much-needed holiday to 'sort ourselves out'. We spent this time putting everything right with God and with each other. We came home exhausted but much more at peace. Also we prayed every day for the gift of a new child. It was then with great excitement two months later that we discovered that Lindsay was pregnant with our second child.

Since our experience, we have set our hearts on praying for couples to conceive and could tell many stories of couples who have either given up hope or have simply reached desperation point and through prayer we have seen God miraculously enabling conception to take place.

So start praying as soon as you can, for God really is involved in every part of conception as Psalm 139 reminds us

'For you created my inmost being; you knit me together in my mother's womb. I praise you because I am fearfully and wonderfully made; your works are wonderful, I know that full well. My frame was not hidden from you when I was made in the secret place. When I was woven together in the depths of the earth, your eyes saw my unformed body.'

As a church we hold 'prayer showers' for women as they are about to have their babies. One of the women in the church, usually someone with pastoral oversight of the expectant mother, invites a group of about 12 women around about two weeks before the birth date. The father-to-be usually arranges to be out and in fact an alternative for men is now emerging as we gather together for our own support evening. The prayer shower begins with some worship and perhaps a reading from Scripture. Then there is an opportunity for the expectant mother to share all her concerns and prayer requests in relation to the forthcoming arrival of her baby. Everyone one then gathers round to pray. The testimonies from these evenings have been very encouraging for everyone concerned.

The greatest prayer for our children is that they would know a relationship with their heavenly Father. Children as young as 3 can understand enough to have a meaningful relationship with Him. Our prayers have been answered and each of our children knows and loves

Jesus. However we know that this is just the beginning and so we continue to pray for them that they would always walk with their heavenly Father.

Pray with them about anything and everything. As young as 1 year old children can copy you praying and very quickly begin to understand the concept of prayer. As they get older and you help them to bring God into everything — anxieties, problems, joys and so on — by encouraging them to pray, they will quickly begin to do it for themselves.

We have always prayed with our children before they go to sleep each night and through this activity have rejoiced with them as we have seen prayers answered.

When Lindsay and I asked our children if they could remember any answers to prayer we were given some lovely examples.

When our children share deep thoughts about things that are troubling them or about ways in which they have been hurt we turn to prayer. We pray at the start of a long car journey, we pray before we eat our food — at home and in restaurants. We try to make prayer the most natural thing in the world.

We have never tried to protect our children from some of the struggles in life. Like all churches we have our share of ups and downs and we pray for many people in our community who are ill, whether or not they come to church. We have also fasted (gone without food for certain periods to help focus our minds on prayer) when we have had a particular desire to hear God for the church or to pray for someone who is particularly ill. Our children, are great prayers and they joined us particularly when a friend, Paul, became ill with cancer. Sadly after a struggle that lasted about 14 months Paul died and we as a family had to go through a time of talking and explaining about life and death. Our children have grown in their prayer life through this and many other similar occasions.

Be open with your children about your own faith. Tell them all that you know about God so that they learn from you. 'Isn't God good!' is a comment we often make referring to a particular activity we might be involved in. On our arrival to our holiday cottage recently we all rushed into the house and the children raced upstairs to see their bedrooms for the next week. 'It's fantastic to be here' our son said. 'Yes isn't God good to provide us with a holiday and a home to come to' was our reply.

One of the things that we love doing as a family is going on walks together especially when they are full of adventure. Recently we went on a walk and the footpath disappeared after only a few fields. The adventure began as we looked for ways to reach our destination and with each new challenge came an opportunity to thank God for his goodness. The lambs in the fields or the birds in the hedgerows, the little waterfalls. All of these provide an opportunity to talk about God and his ways.

We consider the views from the top of hills and the vastness of God's creation, we consider the stars and the sun and the moon. On a visit to the beach on a cold February day, we all wondered at how clever God was to make fish to live in the freezing sea and us to live on the land. 'In fact, isn't it incredible, the way he has made birds to fly, some in cold areas and some in warm. Isn't God amazing, the way he created all of this world. Look at the sea, it's so powerful and God made it,' was my pondering comment! 'Yes and He made sand for us to play with and puddles for us to jump in' came the reply.

We will often talk about our hopes for God's kingdom in our church. We might talk about our prayers and about answers to our prayers. We also share of God's work in other peoples lives, how he has answered a prayer or met a need.

Let them see you reading your Bible and praying so that they know you are really living out what you are talking to them about. Children learn so much from copying and if they see us spending time with God they will want to do the same.

Our children know that Lindsay and I start each day by reading a psalm together in bed and that at other times we might be found on our own with our Bibles. If we set the example, our children, we pray, will follow.

Encourage them to enjoy the Bible themselves. For the older ones, buy them a Bible of their own and some fun Bible teaching notes to help them understand what they are reading. Doing it with them will let them know that you think it is important. For younger children, a toddler Bible or very simple notes are good. Read them Bible stories and talk to them about how they apply God's Word to their own lives.

There are so many good Bibles available today and many are designed so that we can read a story a night to our children. In these early years when children love their parents to read to them each night, try reading a regular story and then a Bible story. This means that they will be getting two stories and learning about God at the same time.

Let them see you worshipping in church. At all times we are to give the lead. I often encourage our worship group in this. 'If you worship rather than trying to get everything musically perfect then others will follow'. And it is so true. The same is true in families. If we make worship of God a priority in our lives and an important activity both in and out of church then our children will do the same. We might often talk about the songs we sing in church and explain why we sing what we do. We also talk about why we worship God and why it's important to us.

Encouraging children to listen to children's worship tapes and learn the songs with them is another great activity that helps great truths from the Bible to be learnt.

Read books to them with a Christian message. Fill their minds with good things. There are many good books around and we can encourage our children to enjoy them by reading with them or buying them as little presents.

Worship together as a family. Read the Bible together and talk about it. Allow opportunity for everyone to talk and to share what they would like prayer for and then pray for each other. Use these times as opportunities for strengthening and encouraging your children's own personal relationship with God. Family Time is a great time to do this.

Nothing we do for our children is more important than encouraging them to live their lives for God each day. It's as they open their hearts to the riches of His grace that they will know that peace that passes all understanding. All of the teaching that we do, all of the encouraging that we engage in are secondary to a relationship with God, for then, like us, each child of God will choose to live life His way.

BIBLE REFERENCES USED IN THIS CHAPTER

Philippians 4:8,9
Proverbs 13:20
1 Corinthians 15:33
Proverbs 9:7–10
Psalm 139:13–16a

Recommended reading for this chapter

Power of a Praying Parent by Stormie Omartian, Kingsway Publications Ltd

Questions for discussion groups

1 Who or what had the greatest influence on you when you were a child, besides your family? Was this a good thing or not?

2 Our children don't just react passively to their influences, they respond as well. How does this encourage you?

3 We have heard that a personal relationship with Jesus makes a big difference in the way our children respond to their influences. Was this true for you as a child and how do you feel it made a difference for you? Is it true for your children now and if so, can you share of ways in which you have sought to encourage them in their relationship with God?

Application points...

1 Review the "Who is influencing our children?" chart and think about any changes you may need to make.

2 Consider your children's relationship with God. Do they know Him as Father and Friend? If not, look at how you might encourage your children to develop that relationship. Spend time praying that God will reveal himself to your children.

6

HE WHO SOWS RIGHTEOUSNESS REAPS A SURE REWARD... (Proverbs 11:18)

I guess that we all dream dreams and have hopes for our children. I wonder what some of your dreams and hopes are for your children?

First on the list of some of the things that we really hope for our children would be that we hope and pray that they come to know Jesus as their Saviour. A relationship with God has changed our own lives so dramatically, in a positive way, and it is wonderful to think that our children might receive the same blessing in their lives.

Next would be that they find a partner who they can share life with. More than that, that they will find a partner for life. To think that they might find someone with whom they can share their lives, someone who will help them reach their potential in life. We hope for a person who will be with them in the ups and downs of life, sharing in sorrows and joys. We pray that they will find someone that they can laugh with as well as cry with. We especially pray that none of them would have to go through the pain of divorce or separation.

We pray for them to have children to enjoy. We pray that they will know the pleasure that we know in having children. We hope that they have sandy beach holidays, walks in the woods, family bike rides and fun in the park.

We don't wish financial riches for our children but just enough to live life and be comfortable, so probably a career or job that they find satisfying would be next on the list. We pray that they will be satisfied in their work as well as in their recreation.

We must ask ourselves: is there any way we can help these hopes and dreams to become reality?

This chapter is all about the preparation we put into our children's lives. If we are to bring up children who are not just outwardly obedient, having learnt to do the right things mechanically, but who will go on to live godly lives, choosing to do what is morally right rather than wrong, then we will need to train their hearts. Our aim as parents is to bring up children whose lives are an external expression of a changed heart. This is of course what we are all trying to do when we become Christians. We seek to live lives that honour God so that through our lives others will see something of God.

In the previous chapter we saw the importance of introducing our children to Jesus, of encouraging them to have a relationship with God right from the start. And we saw that one of the benefits of this relationship will mean that they will have hearts which are open and respond positively to all that we seek to teach them.

In addition to nurturing them in their faith, we need to be constantly placing in their hearts the values which God upholds and which we find in the Bible.

Family Values

As we said in chapter 4, every family has values — particular standards, attitudes, ideas and beliefs that affect how that family operates. Are material possessions important or do friendships and family relationships have greater value? What causes Mum and Dad to 'go mad' and what goes by without them even commenting? Is keeping the house tidy too important to allow friends home for pizza and coke or are people welcome in your home at any time? What attitudes do the children grow up with? Is a relationship with God central to family life or does life go on from week to week without reference to Him? Answers to these sorts of questions give a clue to family values.

What values are we passing on to our children? If we are going to be placing them in our children's hearts we need first to have identified what they are. Sometimes they are so in-built that we live them out without being conscious of what they are. Also, our values can change. Especially if we became Christians in adulthood, it might be that we gradually had to adopt a new set of values because those we grew up with were not in keeping with what we found in the Bible.

What values did you grow up with in your family? What values do you have now? It might help to look at this list and see whether or not you agree with them.

- God is number one in our lives. No person or thing is more important than Him. We should make time to worship Him and should never speak in a way that is dishonouring to Him.
- Family relationships are important, especially the ones between parents and children.
- It is wrong to take another person's life.
- Marriage is a God-given thing and is the only right place for sex.
- We should always pay for what we want to own unless we are given it as a gift. Stealing is always wrong.
- Honesty and truth are very important values. It is wrong to tell lies, or put someone else in a bad light.
- It is wrong to be jealous of what other people have and think that you should have it as well. People are more important than possessions.

- We should respect the law and honour all those in authority over us. Breaking the law will generally hurt others in the end.

The Bible says, 'See to it that no one takes you captive through hollow and deceptive philosophies, which depend on human tradition and the basic principles of this world rather than Christ.' (Colossians 2:8) We must ask ourselves wether the values of our home are based on human tradition and the basic principles of this world or on God and His Word.

You may notice that this list is based on the Ten Commandments (Exodus 20:1–17) and if you find you do agree with what it contains, then the chances are that many if not all of your Family Values are based on God and His Word.

We want to do all we can to place these Family Values into the hearts of our children. We want to give them a framework for life. We want to place into their hearts values that are godly, honest and biblical. How can we do this?

The heart is very closely linked with the work of the conscience and in fact the Bible speaks of the conscience in the New Testament (30 times) and of the equivalent 'heart' in the Old Testament (860 times).

Before I (Mark) became a Christian, I had very different values from the ones I now hold. Therefore my value system has changed. I have chosen to adopt Christian values. So before I was a Christian I would not have considered obeying the law as particularly important. It was more a matter of seeing what could I get away with.

We are made in the image of God and in each of us there is a conscience. God has made us with a basic sense of right and wrong, of good and evil, but we are able to adapt and shape our value system. And while our children are young, we have the opportunity to place in their hearts, in their conscience, God's value system.

Psalm 119:11 sums it up *'I have hidden your word in my heart that I might not sin against you.'* And just as David had hidden God's word in his own heart, we can 'hide' God's word in our children's hearts.

What an exciting prospect! Let's look more closely at how we can shape the conscience with God's values, values which if we so choose can be our own family values.

The Value Warehouse

Psalm 119:11 The action — David hid something
The object — The Word of God
The place — The heart
The reason — in order to maintain a right relationship with God

So we see that the heart is the area in which values or principles for life are placed and stored. It receives, stores and governs instruction. It's like a 'value warehouse', a bit like when you buy something in Argos. You tell the cashier what you are looking for and he goes through the computer to see if it is in stock in the warehouse. If it is, someone goes and collects it from the correct bay and shelf and brings it to you at the counter[1].

The Bible says in Deuteronomy 6:6 'These commandments that I give you today are to be upon your hearts. Impress them on your children.' We, the parents, are to manage the warehouse by filling the 'shelves' of our child's conscience with moral content. We place in our children's hearts the values of honesty, respect, fairness, wisdom, honour, gentleness and patience in order that they then have resources to draw from when they have moral choices to make.

However, just because a child knows right from wrong, doesn't necessarily mean they will choose right! That is why we stressed in the last chapter the importance of encouraging our children to open their hearts to Jesus. As

God grows the fruits of the Spirit in our children, such things as self-control begin to manifest themselves and it is only then, with hearts that want to follow Jesus, that our children will choose right rather than wrong.

Value search system

So we place into the hearts of our children Christian values. We teach them the ways of God. We input good and honest conduct as exhibited in our lives. It is then from this store of knowledge that our children are able to find answers to almost everything they will be involved in in life.

We are faced with new decisions every day. Whether we're out shopping, in the office or watching television, we are constantly confronted with ethical issues which require us to make the right moral choices. For each new

situation we meet, a search system comes into play, scanning the value warehouse, our conscience, for the corresponding value. If a corresponding value is found, we can apply it to the situation. If on the other hand no corresponding value is found, the process ends and we take no action.

Here is an example...

It's Saturday afternoon and, in order to give the children some fresh air, you've wandered into town and find yourself in the children's section of the local book shop. You need to buy a present and as you browse deciding what to buy you don't notice until it's too late that your 2 year old has managed to reach out of her buggy, grab one of the books off the shelf and has torn two of the pages in it. Hurriedly you take it from her, close it up while looking over your shoulder to check that no one is looking, pop it back on the shelf and surreptitiously make for the door.

It's as you are leaving that your value search system comes into play and you begin asking yourself whether you should really be walking away from the book your child has just ruined.

And so begins the search up and down the 'shelves' of your conscience or 'value warehouse' and comes back with the biblical principle that if you damage or destroy someone else's property it must be replaced or paid for (Exodus 22:1–15).

Your conscience tells you that you need to act and so you return to the shop, find the book from the shelf, go to the sales assistant and pay for the damaged book.

It is these values that we put into our children's hearts. If there were no value referring to property in your warehouse your search would have come back empty and you would have gone home £3.99 better off.

We had a personal example of this value search system in our family a while back. We went shopping in Richmond and having parked in the car park Lindsay went to buy the ticket and duly put it on the car. As we walked to the shops our daughter said, 'why do we have to pay to park there, it's not fair'. Our initial reaction was to say that if we don't pay we might get a fine. But then Lindsay's value search system came into play and she started to look for the moral reason why we pay to park in car parks. Lindsay came up with the value from Scripture 'You shall not steal' and went on to explain that that land belongs to someone else and if we park on it without paying that is like stealing from them, regardless of whether anyone found us out or not.

You will find that as you seek to live this way, people will probably think you are mad. Our society is morally dull and many people have no experience of these biblical values. Some time ago, Lindsay took the children into the Body Shop to do some shopping. On arriving home from their trip she realised that our son, who was then two, had taken one of the hair slides from the shelf and had brought it home without us noticing. When we discovered it, our oldest daughter said, 'Oh Mummy. We must take that back. We haven't paid for it.' Lindsay had to agree with her and so at the next opportunity we called in to the Body Shop to return the hairslide. Of course, the assistant was completely dumbfounded. She clearly thought we were unusual, to say the least, but also admitted to thinking that what we had done was right, even though she might not have done that herself!

How do we input these values?

In their very early years we will be directing our children by using quite a few negatives. So we find ourselves saying 'No' or 'Don't touch' several times a day. At this stage our parenting may be typified by lots of restrictions, warnings and consequences. This is because before the age of about three, a child doesn't have the moral capacity to understand reason, nor the awareness of how his actions relate to those around him. From around three, however, we need to make the transition to a much more positive form of shaping.

Now we begin to input positively into our child's conscience. This is typified by instruction, encouragement and reinforcement. We are now looking to move the child's motivation for doing the right thing from 'we might get a fine if we don't buy a car park ticket... ' to the love of righteous living, 'it is the right thing to do to pay for our car parking.'

This will constantly involve us in providing the reason 'why' in answer to many of their questions and as an accompaniment to our instructions.

So how does this change of approach manifest itself in the family? Here is an example. We have a rule in our house that when the children wake up in the morning, they stay in their beds and read quietly (other than going to the loo, of course!) until Mum and Dad get up and the day begins. Our older three children (9, 6 and 4) know the reason behind this: if they were to get up and play, the noise would wake those who are still sleeping and the morning would start badly for everyone.

Not long ago, our youngest daughter, then about 2 1/2, moved from her cot into a bed. She was too young to understand the reasoning behind the rule for staying in bed in the morning. And so we made it clear to her that if she got out of bed without permission, she would have to go back into her cot. She has learnt to stay in her bed through fear of the humiliation of returning to her cot!

In addition, our other daughter, who shares the same room, stays in bed as far as possible in order not to make it difficult for her little sister.

So it is training through negative consequences that has taught our youngest child to do what the other three do because they understand the reason why.

In time our children should begin to do things because

they are the right things to do. The value warehouse begins to act by itself. And we have discovered that they also start to explain to each other why a certain course of action is right! Then you really feel you're getting somewhere.

Making the transition. We must stress how important it is to make the transition between negative and positive training. Failure to do so could lead to frustration, as our children won't understand the reasons behind what you are requiring of them.

A healthy conscience is what we are looking to develop in our children. A healthy conscience is marked by an attitude of 'I ought to do this because it is right', motivated by the love of righteous living. Obedience becomes attractive simply because it is the right thing to do.

An unhealthy conscience is marked by an attitude of 'I must or else I'll be punished'. Here the motivation for obedience is fear of punishment (eg. our own initial reason for paying to park in the car park). If children grow up with an unhealthy conscience we are preparing them to live a life in which they constantly either feel guilty or fear feeling guilty should they get something wrong. They will always be on the verge of doing wrong.

This unhealthy conscience may have developed because the child never knew unconditional love from his parents: he may have felt he had to earn their love through good behaviour. Or maybe the parents heaped guilt on the child's shoulders if he misbehaved: so he has learnt to behave in order to avoid feeling guilty. Or maybe the parents didn't input good biblical values and explain the reason for requiring them.

We need to bring up our children to be confident in themselves of what is or isn't the right thing to do in a given situation, and to do it not through fear of guilt or punishment but through a desire to live life as God intended.

As we conclude, let's ask ourselves these questions: What values are we writing on our children's hearts? How are we writing them? Do we adhere to biblical values ourselves and encourage them in our children, stressing the value of others? Our children's response is a reflection of ourselves. Is the love of Jesus in our hearts evident to others from the way we live our lives?

BIBLE VERSES USED IN THIS CHAPTER

Colossians 2:8
Exodus 20:1–17
Psalm 119:11
Exodus 22:1–15
Luke 19:8

Acknowledgements

1 Based on an idea from *Growing Kids God's Way* by Gary & Ann Marie Ezzo, Growing Families International Press, 1993.

Recommended Reading for this chapter

God's Top Ten by J John, Kingsway Publications Ltd

Questions for discussion groups

1 Are you aware of values you grew up with, either positive or negative? What part do they play in adult life?

2 What values are we putting into our children's hearts and how are we doing that?

3 Think about your own conscience? Is it healthy? Are you someone who responds from guilt or because it is the right thing to do?

4 How does it encourage you to know that we can help our children's lives by shaping their conscience?

Application Points

1 Look for opportunities to explain the biblical reason 'why' when children ask questions about everyday activities.

2 Try to be aware of your own responses to situations and see if you can provide a biblical basis for your decisions.

3 Review your relationship with God. Ask yourself, am I setting the example I want my children to follow?

7

WHO'S IN CHARGE?!

We shall now begin to look at the whole area of discipline. Inevitably, this is a subject that arouses many different emotions and opinions which is why we need to be absolutely sure where we are getting our direction and teaching from. As we have said before, we need to be consistent and parent to a standard. It helps to have a thought out, sustainable way of approaching discipline, and one that has been thought through in the cool light of day rather than grasped at in a split second when we're faced with a conflict situation with our children. We can't afford to try a bit of this and a bit of that, taken from the latest magazine or television programme. As Christians, we must get our direction from the Bible.

It is unfortunate that the word *discipline* has lost its

proper meaning today. It has come to imply punishment or smacking. The discipline that is talked of in the Bible is much more than this. Its focus is on training the heart.

Many parenting models revolve around shaping the environment of the child so that he can develop naturally. The parenting that we see in Scripture encourages us to reach and shape the hearts of our children.

Proverbs 23:15,16	'My son, if your heart is wise, then my heart will be glad, my inmost being will rejoice when your lips speak what is right'
Proverbs 23:19	'Listen, my son, and be wise, and keep your heart on the right path'
Luke 6:45	'The good man brings good things out of the good stored up in his heart'
Proverbs 22:15a	'Folly is bound up in the heart of a child.'

It seems then that the untrained heart of a child contains folly. But a trained heart is full of wisdom. The parents' job, as we see it, is to give instruction to our children so as to transform their hearts from ways of folly to the wise ways of God.

Proverbs 22:6 says:	'train up a child in the way he should go and when he is old he will not depart from it.'
Proverbs 1:7–9 says:	'The fear of the Lord is the beginning of knowledge, but fools despise wisdom and discipline. Listen, my son, to your father's instruction and do not forsake your mother's teaching. They will be a garland to grace your head and a chain to adorn your neck.'

It seems that if a child is going to learn, to be trained, it is our job to instruct. This is the purpose of discipline and when looked at in this broader context it becomes an area of exciting opportunity rather than one of tension and stress.

Now although verbal instruction will be the starting point of discipline, it is not the only way a child will learn. There will be other ways such as the obvious correction and appropriate consequences along with tangible incentives, rewards, encouragement and affirmation, which we will go into in the next chapter. But for now we will focus on the whole area of obedience and how this manifests itself in our families.

The Bible speaks of children being obedient to their parents...

Ephesians 6:1	'Children, obey your parents in the Lord for this is right'.
Colossians 3:20	'Children, obey your parents in everything, for this pleases the Lord.'

Why though, should our children obey us? If we know the answer to this question then we can have confidence in our parenting. I'm sure that you, like us, have often seen a parent almost pleading with a child to either come home from a party or to put their coat on ready to go out. Why should our child put their coat on when asked? Why should they do as we ask? What gives us as parents the right to govern in our families? If we can't answer these questions we'll be tentative and insecure in carrying out our role as parents. If we are unsure about the nature and extent of our authority, our children will miss out. They will never know what to expect from us because the ground rules will be constantly changing.

These days parenting goals are often based upon immediate comfort and convenience. If we require obedience, say, because we feel stressed, then obedience of children is reduced to parental convenience. But if we can have a clear understanding of what the Bible teaches about parenting and can then put into practice this teaching with our children it will be enormously helpful.

As a parent we have authority for one simple reason: because God calls us to be in authority over our children's lives. We have the authority to act on behalf of God. We act at His command and we have a responsibility to shape our children's lives not as pleases us but as pleases Him. All we do must be done from this standpoint. We must undertake all our instruction, care, nurture and correction because this is God's calling. There is much in the Bible to back this up

Our children have been entrusted to us by God to be brought up to know and love Him. The teaching in the Bible helps us to do just that. Proverbs 13:1 'A wise man heeds his father's instruction.'

Ephesians 6:4 commands us to bring up our children in the training and instruction of the Lord. This is not simply a command to train and instruct. It is a command to provide the training and instruction of the Lord. In other words to function on God's behalf.

And this whole thing is liberating because we, just like our children, have no choice in the matter of discipline. As Christians we have chosen to live in submission to God and He has called us, as parents, to be in charge of our children. So when we direct and correct our children we are acting not out of personal desire, but out of obedience to God. We don't need to wonder if it's OK to be in charge. That was God's intention when he gave us our children.

A while ago Lindsay was out collecting one of our children from school and she observed this. A child climbed up onto the school gate. 'Get off the gate' said the mother. The child didn't respond. 'Get down!' said the mother again. No response. 'Get down!' 'But I want a ride,' said the child. 'Oh, you want a ride. All right.' Just

a simple incident, the like of which happens hundreds of times each day, probably. In our culture, parents have begun to take the role of advisor rather than parent. If our children would prefer to do something other than what we have asked them to do, that is fine. The child makes the decisions, the parent suggests options. And often our children have so much choice that by the time they reach 10 or 11 they are their own bosses and parents have very little control at all.

So, as we look at this area of obedience, we must acknowledge our responsibility and see ourselves not as care-providers but as parents who are in charge.

And the benefits for our children are many. Firstly, for our children to learn obedience helps them to fulfil the commandment 'Honour your father and mother'.

Second, to learn obedience is crucial if we are to encourage our children towards their own relationship with God. It will be through obedience to God that they will learn to hear His voice and respond to Him.

Third, to live in obedience to parents brings safety for our children. In Ephesians 6:1–3, God has drawn a circle of great blessing. It says, 'Children, obey your parents in the Lord, for this is right.' 'Honour your father and mother' — which is the first commandment with a promise — 'that it may go well with you and that you may enjoy long life on the earth.' Children are to live within the circle of submission to parental authority. Within that circle things will go well. Obedience to you is for their sakes. They are the direct beneficiaries of honouring and obeying Mum and Dad. The disobedient child has moved outside the place of blessing. The circle of blessing is a place of safety. By implication, being outside that circle is a dangerous place to be.

And fourth, children who have been taught and encouraged in obedience will respond well to authority in general, easily receiving correction later in life and will thus grow in wisdom and understanding (Proverbs 15:5, 29:15). The Bible is full of references relating to authority. Hebrews 13:17a says 'Obey your leaders and submit to their authority', Romans 13:1 says 'Everyone must submit himself to the governing authorities, for there is no authority except that which God has established. The authorities that exist have been established by God.' 1 Peter 2:13–14 says, 'Submit yourselves for the Lord's sake to every authority instituted among men; whether to the king, as the supreme authority, or to governors, who are sent by him to punish those who do wrong and to commend those who do right.'

The Bible then, upholds authority. But probably, if we are honest, many of us may not find coming under authority the easiest thing in the world. We like to do our own thing. It doesn't come easily to 'do as we are told.' And yet the Bible makes it clear that we must respect authority and teach our children to do the same.

Authority is needed for order. If it weren't for authority, we would risk our lives every time we went out in the car; we would have no certainty that our savings were safe in the hands of the building society; buying food from the supermarket would become a health hazard and so on.

Also it brings fair play. If we all play by the rules, we honour others and they can enjoy life. If we cheat, others suffer, including ourselves at the end of the day. Here's an example. There is a park, behind our house and it's a place where people like to walk their dogs. The rule is that people must clean up after their dogs and if they do that everyone else can enjoy the park too. If they don't, an unpleasant time is had by all, especially when we get home and have to scrape the dog's mess off four children's shoes!

We need to be teaching our children to obey the rules but we also need to talk to them about why we do that. Firstly, we obey because God says we are to submit to authority, or do as we're told. And secondly, we obey because rules are there to make life more pleasant for everyone and to obey demonstrates the high regard we have for the preciousness of others.

So, how do we fare ourselves when it comes to authority? As we've said already, our children will copy us — they will pick up our attitudes and if we are bolshy about coming under authority, we can expect them to be the same. Lindsay remembers a time at school when she was about 11 when some of her friends thought it was rather funny and clever to get into detention. And just like many other 11-year olds, she copied their attitude. And she remembers arriving home and telling her mother that some of her friends had got detentions and being very flippant about it. But she recalls that her mother didn't react in quite such a flippant way. She was completely appalled. 'Don't you ever get a detention,' she said. 'Daddy and I would not be pleased at all if that happened to you!' Her reaction quite shocked Lindsay but it had a real impact on her. And all of a sudden the importance that her parents placed on the authority of the school and its system of sanctions came right home to her and the whole event was quite sobering!

The basic rule of thumb is that if we want our children to respect authority, we need to respect it too.

Recently, we went to see a film that carried a 12 certificate. I (Mark) went to buy a bag of sweets for us to munch during the film. However, what caught my attention was a mother arguing with the ticket office attendant. Evidently she had tried to buy a ticket for her 11 year old son to see the film but was refused. 'Oh how ridiculous' she kept saying. 'He's nearly 12 so why can't you let him in?' That boy is going to grow up not knowing that it's important for everyone's sake that we abide by the law of the land.

Our children, then, for the reasons we've suggested, are called to be obedient to their parents. But here are a couple of warnings.

1 We must keep humble in our role as God's agents and always be aware that we, just like our children, can fall short (and often do!). We may need to apologise to our children if we, for example, find ourselves venting our anger on our children. The role of correcting and directing doesn't give us an excuse for outbursts of rage!

2 We must note the warning in Colossians 3:21, 'Fathers, do not embitter your children or they will become discouraged.' Parents should not exercise their authority without thought. We must seek to avoid unnecessary exasperation. In all things we should be consistent, warm and encouraging to our children.

With those things in mind, let's look at obedience and see how it works out in the lives of our children.

There will be times when our children will ignore or oppose our reasonable instructions. What can we do? We can teach them how we expect them to respond. So often our children are willing to respond if we will only show them how. We would suggest that the appropriate response for a child to make to a reasonable instruction would be to say 'Yes, Mum' or 'Yes, Dad' and then to act on that instruction straight away.

Sometimes, quite often in fact, we will need to ask our children to do something they are not keen to do! If they respond with complaints about why what we have asked is not fair, or excuses or explanations then they are not, in all honesty, being obedient. Submission means that they obey a request straight away. If our children are able to respond immediately to the request 'Please would you get ready, I want to take you to MacDonalds', then surely they can respond just as quickly to the request 'Please would you tidy your room'!

Our understanding, then, would be that when we say to our child, 'Darling, I want you to go to bed now', there is only one appropriate response. It's not 'I'll go after I finish colouring this page,' or 'Why do I always have to go to bed so early?' It's not to ignore you altogether! The only truly obedient response is to go to bed without delay. And in fact if we accept or expect anything different, we will likely in effect teach our child to be disobedient. We will teach them that obedience isn't a priority.

We believe that we need to aim for first-time obedience on the part of our children. Now, we know that for all of us, that seems a tall order. But in fact, it is likely to be more of a problem for us than it is for our children. Interestingly, our children often respond to their parents' resolve and nothing more. So often it is we, the parents, who unwittingly teach disobedience, whilst desiring obedience. Here are some ways that parents often undermine their own efforts[1]:

1 Parents who threaten and repeat themselves

When we ask our children to do something, do we really expect them to do it? How often do we have conversations such as this …

'Tommy, put your shoes on. Tommy, did you hear me? I asked you to put your shoes on. Tommy, if you don't put your shoes on I'm going to get cross. Tommy, do you want me to get very cross? Tommy, if you are a good boy and put your shoes on, you can have some chocolate. Right, no chocolate for you! Tommy, if you don't put your shoes on I'll smack you! Tommy, put your shoes on!! Right, you've had enough warnings, I'm going to smack you … ' at which point Tommy quickly puts his shoes on and we say 'good boy Tommy.'

Our children know when we really mean what we say. They are born gamblers. They will tiptoe across the line, enjoy being naughty, and then dash back in the hope of not disturbing the sleeping giant, the parent. So, obedience become subjective. Consequences are no longer tied to disobedience, but to the mood and whim of the parent at any particular moment. The threatening and repeating parent fosters a fearful subjective response. The failure of parents to maintain a consistent standard in discipline only serves to lure a child into failure by causing him to think that he will get away with anything.

2 Parents who bribe

We touched on this in our introductory chapter. But it's worth reminding ourselves by asking, am I the sort of parent who barters with my children in order to gain their obedience? Having asked them to clear up their toys with little response, do I then say, 'Listen, if you clear up your room, then you can have an ice-cream'? This will probably get the desired response in the short-term, but if it continues, our children will grow up expecting rewards in return for obedience. What's in it for me? will be their only motivation for obeying. Of course children should sometimes be rewarded for their obedience, but should not be obedient just to get a reward.

3 Parents who negotiate in the midst of conflict

How often do we allow our children to barter with us in the midst of a conflict situation? It might be that the babysitter has just arrived and as you leave you say to your child 'Up to bed at 8.30. No later.' Your child replies with 'Oh, can't it be 9 o'clock, just this once?' And the battle begins! You try to insist on 8.30 because it's school tomorrow and it's been a busy week, but eventually your child wears you down and through sheer embarrassment in the front of the baby sitter you agree to move to 8.45. What has happened? Your child has pushed you into moving the boundary and, because he has succeeded this time he will be even more determined to do the same again next time!

4 Parents who misuse compassion

How often do our children only see and experience our compassion and never our judgement and justice? How will they ever learn to do as they are asked if their disobedience always ends in hugs? We are not being un-loving by insisting that requests by mum and dad are obeyed.

5 Parents who offer too much choice

Do you have days like this one? You get up in the morning and get out your child's blue jumper and trousers and start to dress him. 'Oh I wanted to wear my red jumper!' he says. 'OK' you say. You go down for breakfast and you put his Weetabix in the bowl. 'Oh I want Cornflakes' he says. 'Ok' you say, as it's no trouble to change it. You get to mid morning and you give your child a drink. 'Oh I wanted it in my Thomas cup!' he says. 'OK, here you are.' You get to the supermarket and go to put your child in the trolley. 'I want to walk!' he shouts. 'OK then, I suppose we're not in a hurry.' You go for a walk in the afternoon and before you can catch your breath your child runs off without waiting for you. As he runs in front of a cyclist you shout 'stop' only to see the cyclist almost falling of his bike and your child calling 'But I want to go by myself'. Fortunately no cars are coming but you feel dreadful and *wish* like anything that your child would do as you say.

If we allow our children constantly to make their own choices it is then difficult for them to give up that choice when the crunch comes.

10 tips to help when addressing our children and expecting a response.

What can we do to help our children towards obedience? This is not as difficult as many would think but it does require a willingness to be consistent. We will need to be willing to be strong and swim upstream because it is no longer fashionable either to submit to or to encourage submission to authority. And we will need to adhere to some basic principles of communication.

1 Expect a response. When you speak to your child in a way that requires an answer or action, expect a response. Often we expect no response and therefore that is exactly what we get!

2 Say what you mean and mean what you say. Never ask your child to do something unless you intend it to be carried out. If you give instructions you have no intention of enforcing, you will quickly teach your child to be disobedient.

3 Be careful how you phrase your instruction. Instructions phrased in the form of a question 'Would you like to go to bed now?' are likely to get the answer 'No!' Be firm in the way you give your instructions, e.g. 'It's time for bed now, up you go'.

4 Provide a warning. An instruction that interrupts or ends an activity should be preceded by a warning. This is fair and will prevent you from frustrating your child. Sometimes it is appropriate to give a 5-minute warning. So if you notice that it is approaching bed time and your children are playing a game, give them a warning that they will have to finish in the next 5 minutes. This will help your child to prepare for the instruction to 'Go to bed now'. Obedience will be more attractive if our children know that we are mindful of what they are involved in.

5 Provide a door of escape. You may have given a clear instruction to clear up a bedroom but as fast as it is cleared up a little brother or sister messes it up again. The door of escape is to bring the problem to you so that you can help sort it out.

6 Consider the context. Ask the question 'Is what my child is doing disobedient in this particular context?' So, for example, in our house we have a rule that once the children are in bed they don't get out until we say they can, which will probably be the next morning. We have another rule: when you go to the loo, you flush it after you and put the lid down. That makes it nice for the next person to use. If we were to settle our boys down and then come upstairs and find one of them getting back into bed our first thought might be that he had been disobedient in getting out of bed. But if we asked him what he was doing and he said he had remembered he hadn't flushed the loo earlier so went to the bathroom to flush the loo before going to sleep, then that would alter everything. In these circumstances, the context qualifies the original intent.

7 Be consistent. Teaching obedience requires consistency and the giving of clear instructions. Without clear and consistent instructions our children will be at a loss to know what to do.

8 Get eye contact and a verbal response. E.g. 'Sam, look at Mummy. I want you to go and put your shoes and coat on and wait by the front door.' 'Yes Mummy.' Eye contact helps the child to focus on the instruction and then to process it. A verbal response again helps with processing the instruction.

Sometimes our children will say they didn't hear us. Therefore it is often good to call a child's name first rather than give a straight instruction. E.g....

'Sam!'

'Yes Dad?'

'It's bedtime, son'

9 Don't be too quick to repeat yourself. Once your children know that you expect to have to say something only once they will quickly learn that you won't say it again (unless of course they genuinely haven't heard). And it's amazing how, once you have resolved not to repeat yourself, the children learn to respond much more quickly.

10 Remember our example. Whatever is right for the children must also be seen as right for us. E.g. In our house we take off our shoes at the front door. The children are very quick to notice if we don't take off our shoes!

Finally, we must expect conflict. All children will constantly come up against situations where their own desires are in conflict with our instruction. Obedience is a lesson that we all have to learn and as we know from our own lives, that learning curve continues throughout life. The more willing we are to be consistent in our teaching of this in our own families the quicker our children will learn obedience and ultimately everyone will benefit. Inconsistency will simply bring frustration for your child. And since conflict is inevitable in every family it is helpful to view conflict not as a negative thing but as an opportunity to move our children forward in the right direction. For our younger children (4 and younger, say) when conflict arises, it can give us the opportunity, to establish in their minds our requirement of first-time obedience. For our older children, rebellious or inappropriate behaviour can provide an opportunity for us to help them to understand that what needs to happen is a change of heart.

As wise, thinking parents, then, we have the power to choose whether we allow negative behaviour to be detrimental to our children or rather advantageous, a means of taking them closer to God's ideal. What an exciting thing conflict can be when we see it like that!

The opportunity to appeal

Our children are not machines. They have thoughts and ideas of their own and it is important that we guard ourselves against becoming authoritarian in our parenting. So, once our children have grasped that they are under

our authority and can't always do as they like (probably around the age of 5), it is a good idea to teach them that it is fine to appeal about what you have instructed, as long as it is done respectfully. This is a good thing because...

a) We may have spoken in a hurry without thinking about what we were saying. It allows us to change our mind about something, which in retrospect is inappropriate.

b) It protects our children from feeling that they are always in a no-win situation. To know that Mum and Dad will listen to them and reconsider what we have said if necessary and appropriate is a good safety valve.

So, for example, you might have asked your child to come and lay the table for tea but hadn't realised that he was almost at the end of a game of 'Guess who?' with his brother. To come straight away will be very frustrating for him, yet not to come will amount to disobedience. At times like this, it is beneficial for everyone if our children can appeal about what we have asked.

We would encourage our children to appeal like this:

a) On hearing our instruction they begin to act straight away.
b) They appeal respectfully and not in a whine.
c) Should their appeal be unsuccessful, they accept graciously.

So to take the above example to its conclusion, your child might simply come to you and say, 'Mum, we've almost finished a game of 'Guess who?', would you mind if we finish it before I lay the table?' And in 9 cases out of 10 that would be fine.

Even better, we as parents can be thinking ahead, weighing up what we are about to instruct and checking ourselves as to whether it is necessary and appropriate. So, for example, your child may be reading in bed and it is time for lights out. You could say 'it's time for lights out now', in which case you would expect your child to turn out the light and settle down. Or you could say 'How many more pages to the end of that chapter? Just a page and a half? Ok, finish the chapter and then turn out your light.' This is so much kinder and more thoughtful, so much more in keeping with the way God treats us, and it also shows our children a better example of how to treat others.

A point to note... it can be so tempting, when we have obedient children, to choose to say 'no' to our children's requests, simply because it is more convenient for us. Let's not say 'no' when the answer could just as easily be 'yes'.

Very young children

The earlier we start this obedience training the better, in fact as soon as they begin to deliberately disregard our instructions. At nine months, our daughter would crawl to us when called. A few months later she had her own ideas. But we persisted and her disobedience always brought negative consequences. So she came through it and learnt to come when we call. Similarly even before they can talk, we can require a response, even if it is a nod and a grunt! We can say it ourselves — 'Yes Mummy' — and very quickly they will copy.

We would encourage you to set limits and boundaries right from the start, in other words don't give your baby freedoms which you may later regret. The purpose of limiting our children is not to take away their freedom to explore but to give them freedom within manageable limits, according to how much they can understand. A child with more freedom than he can handle, or more right of access than he can cope with will get himself into trouble. A child cannot enjoy freedom without surrendering some of it.

Don't be afraid to say 'no' to your baby. 'No' simply defines the necessary boundaries. The key to setting limits for your little one is not in controlling his environment by removing everything, but by training him to

your voice. If your child touches something that is out of bounds, tell him 'No' firmly. If he persists you could repeat the 'no' with a squeeze on the wrist or a smack on the hand. If he still persists you may remove him from the tempting object and give him something else to play with or isolate him to his cot for a while.

A little tip: we've noticed that if we say 'no' to our daughter and stand there waiting for her to stop doing whatever she is doing, she will very likely persist, trying to lure us into a power struggle. But if we say 'no, don't touch' and then walk away she will almost always stop. It's as though our presence extends the conflict, whereas if we move away, she can then surrender without losing face.

Sometimes young children, on hearing the word 'no', will throw a tantrum. It is unlikely that a child will get through the early years without having a few tantrums but our children do need to learn that there are appropriate ways of expressing emotion and kicking and screaming isn't one of them! Proverbs 25:28 says, 'Whoever has no rule over his own spirit is like a city broken down, without walls.' If we have no self-control we are vulnerable emotionally.

The way we, as parents, deal with tantrums will have a great bearing on whether they become frequent. If the tantrum is successful, in other words if it enables the child to get what it wants, it will probably recur. If, on the other hand, it doesn't achieve the desired result the first time, it is less likely to be repeated.

So what can we do when a tantrum occurs? If it is a tantrum born out of frustration, because the child can't physically manage to make the Lego model he has in his mind's eye, then we need to be sympathetic and help out if required. However, if it is clearly a temper tantrum it's a good idea to remove the child to a cot or if you're in public strap him into a buggy away from people until he has calmed down. For a child of more than about 2 1/2, he will need to know that once he has calmed down there will be a consequence to his tantrum. This will help him not to repeat it in the future. Also, if left to pass uncorrected, the underlying attitude will remain and may manifest itself later in rudeness, defiance or similar.

Finally, as we have said throughout the book, we are looking to reach our children's hearts. Our aim is not to focus on behaviour, but rather to see behaviour as an indication of what is goiing on in our children's hearts. Training our children to respond to our voice the first time we speak means training them in God's standard of obedience. And this will prepare them firstly to carry out God's command, 'Honour your father and mother that it may go well with you and that you may enjoy long life on the earth' and thus know God's blessing on their lives. And secondly having learnt how to submit willingly to authority, they will be ready as Christians living in relationship with the living God to hear his voice of instruction and wisdom and obey it. Only then will they come to know and experience the fruit of obedience — true freedom in Christ.

BIBLE VERSES USED IN THIS CHAPTER

Proverbs 23:15,16	Proverbs 23:19
Luke 6:45	Proverbs 22:15a
Proverbs 22:6	Proverbs 1:7–9
Ephesians 6:1	Colossians 3:20
Proverbs 13:1	Ephesians 6:4
Proverbs 15:5	Proverbs 29:15
Hebrews 13:7	Romans 13:1
1 Peter 2:13–14	Colossians 3:21
Ephesians 6:1–3	Proverbs 25:28

Acknowledgements

1 Based on ideas taken from *Growing Kids God's Way* by Gary and Anne-Marie Ezzo

Questions for discussion groups

1 As a child, how were you expected to respond to your parents' requests? Was obedience a part of life in your childhood home?

2 What is our response now when we are required to submit to authority, the law, for example? Do we do it willingly?

3 Do you relate to the parent who threatens, repeats themselves, bribes, negotiates in conflict or allows too much choice? What are your experiences?

4 Children often rise to the level of expectation of their parents. Many parents expect little and receive just that. What is your response to this?

5 What are your thoughts on the subject of first-time obedience? Is it part of your experience and if not, do you see it as an achievable or desirable thing?

6 God has given us responsibility for the disciplining of our children. How do you respond to this?

Application points...

1 Spend time this week working on first time obedience, putting into practice the suggestions for success. If you have younger children, try making a game out of your child coming the first time he is called with a 'yes, Mummy' or a 'yes Daddy'.

2 Try giving a 5-minute warning before giving instructions and see how it makes a difference to your child's response.

3 Explain to your older children how to appeal respectfully about what you have asked them to do. See if it makes a difference to their co-operation.

8

A QUESTION OF DISCIPLINE

In this chapter we begin to look at how discipline can be broken down into different areas. You may remember that in the previous chapter we were saying that it is unfortunate that the word *discipline* has lost its proper meaning today. It has come to imply punishment or smacking. But we believe that discipline is much more than this. Its focus is on training the heart and will therefore consist of a number of different approaches and courses of action, some of which are positive and encouraging and some corrective. Both are needed if we are to be consistent and fair.

As we discuss this whole area of discipline, we need to keep in mind the importance of parenting with a long-term aim. By this we mean that we are not disciplining for the moment, we are not just responding to a situation in order to resolve a crisis, but are looking to be consistent in what we do in order to reach our children's hearts. What is their motive for doing what they are doing? Have we given them proper instruction? Do they know what they are meant to be doing and why?

As we have said, we can all train our children to behave in robot-like ways by punishing them when they misbehave. Our aim, though, is to use discipline in order to reach a point where our children know what is right and therefore desire to do it.

We need to start by distinguishing between skills and behaviour.

1 SKILLS

As we all know, the Christian life in itself requires discipline on the part of every believer. Richard Foster in his book 'Celebration of Discipline' outlines many of the spiritual disciplines we'll need to work at if we're to find true fulfilment and inner peace.

In the same way there are some positive disciplines or skills that our children will need to learn. Skills are not behavioural issues and so do not have a corrective side to them. They are abilities given by God such as riding a bike or learning to swim which need discipline if they are to be acquired. We can help our children to acquire them, chiefly through encouragement and praise.

Children love to be praised for their achievements and the satisfaction of receiving that praise is a great motivator for learning new skills. This sort of confirmation encourages their hearts. Praise is so important in encouraging our children to learn a discipline.

Another way to encourage this type of discipline is to give them a tangible incentive to help them work at learning a particular skill. So, for example, our children's granny has told the children that she will give them a pound for every one of their times tables that they can learn. They will be very satisfied when they achieve their target!

We would be very careful not to overuse these tangible incentives and would use them only for learning a skill as opposed to, for example, a kind of 'bribe' for sitting quietly in the supermarket trolley which is, rather, a behaviour issue.

2 BEHAVIOUR

Behaviour is an indication of what is going on inside our child's heart and unlike a skill, is motivated by **encouragement** *and* **correction** and both are needed if discipline is to be truly effective.

Encouragement

There is so much we can do to encourage our children in their behaviour. With forethought we can encourage them by giving them prior preparation so that they have every opportunity of doing the right thing. So often children want to do the right thing but often miss out because they haven't been encouraged to do so.

So for example, as we walk to church on a Sunday morning or as we travel to spend the day with friends we will ask the children, 'What are the rules for being at church?' And they will have great fun seeing how many things they can remember such as sitting quietly in the quiet bits so other people can concentrate, listening to the person at the front, not running around or shouting after the service while people are having drinks or receiving prayer, and so on. As well as reminding them of the rules, this also helps them to own what they have said and so helps them in carrying out what they have spoken about.

We then also have the joy of praising them for remembering all the rules and after church we can praise them again for doing so well. Sometimes, if they have done really well on a particular day we might surprise them with a treat but we would keep it to a minimum and only offer it afterwards and not beforehand as a kind of 'carrot' or bribe to encourage good behaviour. Our reason for this is because if their motivation for behaving well is a tangible reward, we have lost our focus of reaching their hearts!

Correction

Sometimes, as we parents know only too well, encouragement isn't always enough and our children who are human, just as we are, miss the right path and get themselves into trouble! Then comes the need for correction.

There are several references to correction in the Bible. Here are some verses.

Proverbs 22:15	'Folly is bound up in the heart of a child, but the rod of discipline will drive it far from him'
Proverbs 29:15	'The rod of correction imparts wisdom, but a child left to himself disgraces his mother'
Hebrews 12:11	'No discipline seems pleasant at the time, but painful. Later on however, it produces a harvest of righteousness and peace for those who have been trained by it'

Correction is clearly an integral part of discipline. There will be times when it hurts us very much to correct our children and we may be tempted to let things pass. But we believe that just as God disciplines us, His children, we are to discipline our own children and we shouldn't shrink from that responsibility in order to make life easier for ourselves. Proverbs 13v24 says 'He who spares the rod hates his son, but he who loves him is careful to discipline him'. Whether we take 'the rod' literally or not will be discussed later in the chapter! It is a loving parent who seeks to discipline his child wisely and thoughtfully.

We need to consider the motivation behind a child's particular action before we consider correction. Was it accidental or intentional? Was it done out of childish innocence, or childish thoughtlessness or deliberate naughtiness ? The way in which we answer this question will determine the form of correction needed.

When our children behave badly it is not always a result of a rebellious heart. Sometimes it is simply a result of childish innocence. It may be that they don't realise, because they have never been told that what they have done was wrong and therefore it would be unreasonable for us to expect them to get it right. A couple of years ago, we laid some gravel down between our patio and the garden wall. We were very pleased because it neatened up a rather scruffy area of the garden. We weren't so pleased when we went out into the garden to find the children digging in the gravel and moving it to various parts of the garden, including scattering it on the lawn. It was very frustrating for us but as far as the children were concerned it was just a great game. We hadn't told them not to play with the gravel and in childish innocence they were just occupying themselves while they played outside.

Sometimes childish thoughtlessness is the cause. Had they taken the time to think, they would have realised that to do what they did probably wasn't a good idea. Sometimes in the summer our children love to set up camp in the garden. One day we found them dragging all their duvets and pillows with clean covers on out to the garden where they put them on the damp grass with lots of potential for getting them wet and muddy!

Fortunately I found them in time and was able to send them back inside which, admittedly spoilt their game but at least it saved me having to wash all the covers! What they were doing was not rebellious. It was childish thoughtlessness.

We will need great sensitivity and wisdom as we seek to correct our children's childish behaviour. Sometimes we will need to simply point out what has happened and give them proper instruction so that it doesn't happen again and that will be enough.

Sometimes, such as where thoughtlessness is the problem, a light telling-off may be required and maybe a consequence to help them remember as well. Last summer Mark received a hammock for his birthday and set it up in the garden. Our boys asked if they could play in it to which he responded 'yes of course but don't swing too hard or it will collapse'. After about 20 minutes he saw them swinging far too hard in it and explained that the way they were swinging was too hard. He gave them the benefit of the doubt and assumed that they hadn't understood what 'too hard' was. A few minutes later they got carried away again and at this point the hammock collapsed. Although they hadn't deliberately been naughty, their thoughtlessness had finally lead them into trouble and the hammock had to be put away.

Deliberate naughtiness

Sometimes, as we know, children are deliberately naughty. They might be deliberately disobedient such as kicking a football near the house where windows can get broken. Or they might answer back, or refuse to be corrected or comply with what we have asked them to do. There is also indirect defiance such as pretending not to hear, pleading ignorance, sulking or whining.

We all know our own children and we need to respond to deliberate naughtiness according to their general character and age. We need to ask ourselves such questions as, 'have the circumstances not helped Jonny to be obedient?' If you have been waiting in the doctor's surgery for an hour and a half for example, obedience can begin to be less attractive for any child, to say the least! Is he particularly tired, or hungry? Is he acting out of character or is this something that often occurs and really needs dealing with?

One day I (Lindsay) discovered our smallest children sliding on their knees on the polished hall at the back of our church. Of course, I wasn't pleased and talked to them long and hard about the possibility of knocking into people and making holes in their trousers. But on thinking about it afterwards I realised how difficult it sometimes is for them when Mum and Dad spend a very long time talking after church when really they are tired and could do with having their lunch! We need to take things such as these into account!

Also, we need to be careful when giving correction that we don't overdo it. Correction that is heavier than the crime is very disheartening for our children so we need to make sure we are being absolutely fair.

It is quite helpful to break things down as we consider the suitability or otherwise of a particular form of correction. Generally, deliberate naughtiness will fall into the following:

a) small incidents that need a telling off

We are not perfect and nor should we expect our children to be! In fact we are in danger of exasperating them if we pursue perfection. Sometimes our children will do something which they *should* know is naughty or which they were corrected for three months ago but perhaps they have genuinely forgotten or had a momentary lapse! They may know that they have to put their bikes away in the garden shed at the end of the day but have omitted to do it on this occasion. For us, these sorts of things would call for a warning and encouragement not to forget next time!

b) naughtiness that needs more than just a verbal telling off

We would see this as correction for behaviour that is becoming common or warnings that haven't been heeded or past habits that seem to be getting more regular again. For these sorts of things a stronger telling off might be appropriate, accompanied by an enforced temporary break from the activity they are involved in to give them some thinking time. They may then consider what they were doing wrong and hopefully have a 'change of heart'. Sometimes a permanent break from the activity for that day might be called for to help them remember not to do it again.

Our children were given a table football game one Christmas and it is one which needs to be treated with respect otherwise the poles to which the players are attached snap (this has happened once already!). The children know they need to be careful with it and each time they play with it we remind them that if they fight over it or are too rough it will get broken. All of this being the case, should one of them begin to get over-excited with it we might impose a five-minute break, hoping for a re-think and a change of heart. If they were then to continue to mistreat their football game, the result would be a very firm telling off and the removal of the game, probably for a set period, long enough for them to miss it and adopt a new attitude to their game!

Whining is something that will quickly become a habit if left unchecked. Often we tend to switch off from it in order to protect ourselves but if we do that our children will probably persist because eventually we tend to become worn down by it and give in! How often do we hear 'oh I don't *like* these green bits in my lasagne' or 'oh I *hate* having to tidy my room!' and think it is just part of life that we have to put up with?

How can we eliminate whining? Firstly point out that it is becoming a habit and that it is not an acceptable means of communicating. If requests come in a whine suggest your child goes away and has a re-think and comes back and asks properly. If it still persists a stronger form of correction may be needed, as suggested below.

c) behaviour that will need stronger action

Some things, though, will not be corrected with a telling-off or a chance to think things through! There are some incidents that require stronger correction! So if our child has been seriously disobedient, we will need wisdom in order to make a decision about how to deal with it.

There are various options:

Isolation — Children are very social beings and love

being with other children and adults. To be isolated to a cot or bedroom or even to sit on the stairs if it is right away from others removes that privilege and for many is a very effective means of correction.

A smack — Sadly smacking is often approached so aggressively that it is tantamount to physical abuse. We are all aware that the smacking of children by parents has been frowned upon recently. And an article in *The Times* (26/1/99) recently stated 'Following a judgement from the European Court of Human Rights last September the Government accepted that the law which allows parents to use 'reasonable chastisement' must be changed to give children better protection and agreed to enter consultations on such changes.'

However, the truth is that when a parent rants and raves uncontrollably at their child it is every bit as violent and abusive as an out-of-control slap. The problem with out-of-control smacking is that the emotional pain caused by arbitrary, thoughtless 'discipline' is made worse by the physical abuse.

Any punishment given to a child in an un-thought-out, careless or vengeful fashion is abusive.

It is important to acknowledge that the Bible encourages use of 'The rod of discipline' (Proverbs 22:15, 29:15) but it does not command it. It is not an alternative to reaching our children's hearts by teaching them to show love and self-control and to do the right thing. In fact, unless we are actively working at building loving relationships and a strong, secure home as well as encouraging and teaching godly values to our children, then we believe that smacking is not an option. Smacking alone will not result in a changed heart.

Every parent will make up their own mind about whether it is right to smack their child. If we do decide it is an option, what is important is how the smack is given.

Here are a few practical pointers:

- it should be reserved for wilful defiance
- it should be done with consistency and not just dished out on the days when we happen to be in a bad mood. Children are born gamblers and if they are expecting a smack and don't get one, they will try it again
- it should be done in private to maintain the child's dignity and only ever by the parent
- it should only ever sting, never cause physical injury
- most importantly, it should be done in a loving atmosphere, never in anger by an out-of-control parent and the child should understand fully why he is having the smack. The child needs to be reassured of our love beforehand and afterwards and once things have calmed down he needs to know that that is the end of it.

Withdrawal of a privilege — this might include removal of pocket money or treats, not being allowed to stay up late at the weekend, not being allowed to use a favourite toy for a set period, not being allowed to watch a favourite tv programme and so on. We will all know what is appropriate for our own child.

Logical consequences — this ties in closely with withdrawal of a privilege but would be something related to the behaviour. As our children get older they will often respond more readily to logical consequences. So, for example, if a child doesn't come willingly and cheerfully when you pick him up from going to tea with a friend then the logical consequence might be that he doesn't go the next time he is invited.

Alternatively, if your child is never ready on time and drags his heels when it is time for school but is quite able to get himself ready for cubs which he enjoys then you might apply a logical consequence. You might say 'if you can't get ready for school on time then you will have to miss Cubs this week.' If the lateness continues then Cubs will have to be missed for a week or until things improve.

These are not in any particular order and sometimes more than one will be needed. The important thing is that as thinking parents we will need much wisdom as we decide which form of correction is needed. And we should always try to take time to think and pray before we act.

The most important thing to remember in all of this is that our children should never be in any doubt that *we love them unconditionally*, that whatever they do we will always love them. If our children believe we love them, they will respond so much more readily to our discipline, be it encouragement or correction.

Following on from correction come three important processes:

Repentance, forgiveness and restoration

Feeling sorry about something, regretting what you've done, isn't the same as repentance. To repent is to have a shift or change of heart. In other words there is an inner attitude shift or change of heart which will result in an outward change of behaviour. You can regret without repenting (for example the child who is told not to play ball by the neighbour's fence, does so and then the ball goes over. They feel regret as they've lost the ball. But they are not necessarily repentant at having played football near the fence!).

Repentance is important because it has a crucial effect in the restoration of a relationship. Just as in the Christian life we need to repent not just once but daily of the things which spoil our relationship with God, so it is in our relationships within the family. We need to be making our children aware of how their disobedient and selfish acts can spoil their relationships with others in the family.

As we seek to reach our children's hearts with God's ideals, we are looking for evidence of genuine repentance. For children of 4 and upwards, this should be possible. They will be able to see, albeit simplistically, how their actions have spoilt relationships. But also how through genuine repentance those same relationships can be restored. And it's as the members of the family come to appreciate the connection between their actions and their effect on relationships that family unity can be strengthened. And obviously vice versa.

But genuine repentance alone is not enough for the relationship to be restored (which is obviously our ultimate aim). We know that Jesus offers forgiveness through what He did on the cross to anyone who calls out to Him. But in order for that forgiveness to restore our relationship with God, we need to have repented and accepted that forgiveness. Jesus is always there ready to forgive but man must accept God's offer of forgiveness through Jesus before restoration can take place.

And so it is in our family relationships. Our children need to learn that we are ready to forgive them but equally it is their responsibility to ask for that forgiveness. To say sorry is not enough; it acknowledges a mistake. But to ask for forgiveness demonstrates a change of heart. We think this distinction is an important one and we always encourage our children to say 'I'm sorry. Will you forgive me?' when they have been disobedient or when they have fallen out with a brother or sister. And it's interesting how effectively it brings restoration, probably because both have a part to play in the process and there has to be active agreement for it to take place. When there is genuine repentance it is unmistakable and brings a lovely feeling of peace and harmony to the family.

And as we have already said, there may be times when we as parents have to set the example in saying sorry and asking for forgiveness! It works both ways and if we are in the wrong it will be a very powerful thing for our children to hear us say sorry and ask for forgiveness.

There are two acts, which are very powerful in breaking down the relationships within the family and require us to work hard at encouraging repentance and restoration. They are lying and stealing.

Lying has been called 'The ultimate family sin'. It is something we are all capable of 'Even from birth the wicked go astray; from the womb they are wayward and speak lies.' (Psalm 58:3) and it is on the list of things in Proverbs 6 that are an *abomination* to the Lord which means it is something repulsive, disgusting and foul. Why is lying so bad? Because it attacks the bridge of trust which links each family member to the others. If one link is weakened, they are all weakened.

How do we handle it? Consider the age of your child. An under-3-year-old will not understand the impact that his lie has on his relationships. An older child will, though, and so a good first course is to try to get them to be honest by talking to them. If that doesn't work (it often won't!) move to talking generally about the importance of integrity, of the fact that God requires integrity and he knows everything, and also that everyone's relationships benefit from being honest.

If this doesn't work, we should never resort to calling our child a liar. If your child thinks you don't believe him he will be disheartened about your relationship and unmotivated in it. Also, often we become what we are labelled: we don't want to put that onto our children. For your child to know that you refuse to call him a liar will let him see how much you value your relationship and may well encourage him to come clean in the end.

If he really won't come clean then he will get away with it this time but better that than for your relationship to be damaged. Your child will respect you far more for refusing to discipline him when you are not sure what happened. After all, there will be plenty of times when you do know for sure what happened, and then you can respond appropriately.

Consider also the motive behind the lie. Are they doing it to get attention, to escape responsibility, to get accepted, or to copy someone? Getting to the bottom of why your child is not telling the truth will help you to try to correct it. Also consider your child's general level of honesty. Telling a lie in a moment of weakness is different from habitual lying and needs lighter correction.

Obviously lying needs serious attention and probably a punishment. But with that must come lots of communication about the importance of honesty and of ultimate importance is that family relationships are seen to be prized.

Stealing is another thing that attacks the family and again we have to look at the seriousness of the theft before we dish out a punishment. Taking a biscuit from the tin without permission is not the same as taking £10 from Mum's purse. Also the context is important. So taking a cake from the tin is not equal to taking a cake from the baker's shop. Stealing within the family shames the child, stealing outside the family shames the family.

It's worth mentioning that stealing isn't always tangible. You can steal someone's time, or their reputation through gossiping about them. Gossip is another abomination (Proverbs 6:19). Once you have stolen someone's reputation it is very difficult to restore it. That is a wise thing to teach our children, as we talk to them about stealing: we must mind our own business and guard our tongues.

This brings us to another aspect of restoration that is also important. You will remember that after Jesus had visited Zacchaeus the tax collector he was a changed man and he said this: 'If I have taken anything from any man by false accusation, I restore him fourfold'. (Luke 19:8). What we are talking about is personal responsibility. Saying 'I'm sorry' and asking for forgiveness is not enough if you have created a financial liability accidentally or intentionally.

Some while ago now, we borrowed a travel cot from friends for our daughter to use when we went to stay with family. During her afternoon sleep, she managed to undo the side netting of this travel cot and create a rather large hole. We were of course responsible for this and so we ensured that we replaced the travel cot.

To conclude then, if our family relationships are to be meaningful, repentance, forgiveness and restoration are all elements of parental discipline which cannot be neglected. Inevitably in family life there will always be incidents which bring disharmony, but as we seek to teach our children the importance of restoring these relationships, I believe our families will be stronger and our children more secure as a result.

Rev Steve Chalke, the well-known TV presenter says this: 'Discipline should be the framework and encouragement that a loving parent creates for their child in order to help them gradually learn how to control their behaviour, and develop self-discipline. Discipline should be an enabler: a creative force designed to build maturity and consistency, helping children fit into society without being swamped by it. Discipline should give your children the self-control they need to manage what they do, both now and in the future.'[1]

Discipline is far more than punishment. As we consistently seek to put effort into discipline, first we will be required to do far less correcting than other parents and second, as we put effort into shaping our children's hearts we will find ourselves having to concentrate far less on reshaping our children's outward behaviour.

BIBLE VERSES USED IN THIS CHAPTER

Proverbs 22:15
Hebrews 12:11
Psalm 58:3
Luke 19:8
Proverbs 29:15
Proverbs 13:24
Proverbs 6

Acknowledgements

1 *How to Succeed as a Parent,* Steve Chalke, Hodder and Stoughton, 1997

Questions for discussion groups

1 What was your experience of being disciplined as a child? Has this affected your approach now as a parent?

2 How do you respond to the idea of discipline being more than punishment?

3 What are your thoughts about the different stages of correction for deliberate naughtiness? Are there things you hadn't thought about and if so do you see them helping you in the future?

4 How do you respond to the ideas on repentance, forgiveness and restoration? Can you imagine how this might work out in your family?

Application points...

1 Spend time thinking and talking about the way you discipline your children and discuss any changes that you need to make. Begin to implement them.

2 Find an opportunity to encourage your child in a skill this week.

3 Start putting into practice the encouragement that will help your child know how to respond on different occasions. Try, for example, giving him instruction on what is expected of him at the supermarket or at a friend's house.

4 Look out for examples of 'childish innocence' and 'deliberate naughtiness'. Is it easy to spot the difference?

9

ACTIONS SPEAK LOUDER...

One of the central themes of the Bible is summed up in the commandment that Jesus gave, 'Love your neighbour as yourself' (Mark 12:31) and also in Philippians 2:3 where Paul says that we must esteem and regard others better than ourselves.

If we truly want to bring up our children to love and honour God, if we want to be true to ourselves and to God, we have to find ways of living out this command.

We live in a materialistic age where wealth and mater-

ial possessions are given great value. Many people set out to achieve solely for themselves and to look after number one regardless of how that might affect anyone else. In today's society it comes as a great challenge to take Jesus' teaching to love our neighbour as ourselves seriously.

Now, you might think it's obvious how we can value and respect one another; that we all know *how* to do it but it's *doing* it that is the problem because it's so contrary to our selfish human nature and also to our present culture.

But interestingly, from our observation, for our children, doing it is not the problem. Often our children find doing the right thing much easier than we do. Where they fall down is in not knowing what to do in the first place.

A friend told me recently that one day she took her 9 year-old daughter on the bus and was surprised when she didn't stand up to offer her seat to an elderly person who got on at the next stop. 'I signalled to her to get up but she didn't respond at all!' she told me. After they got off the bus my friend questioned her daughter as to why she had been so rude. 'I didn't know you had to get up and offer your seat to an older person' she said. And at that point my friend realised that she was responsible for this error. She had never explained to her daughter that that is the right thing to do and why.

'People matter, things don't' is a great Family Value to hold. It is crucial. But it is meaningless unless our children know and understand how it is worked out in practice. We need to teach our children how they can demonstrate that they value and respect other people in order that those people *feel* respected and valued. It's a bit like the Love Languages (see chapter 2). It's no good just knowing that you love someone. For love to be real it has to be expressed tangibly and felt by the other person.

So we're going to look at how we can help them to grow in the attributes of love and respect and demonstrate in their everyday lives that others are precious to them.

1. Our children's relationship with God

Obviously, by its very nature, this relationship is very different from the others we shall cover but it is important to look at it because it will become, we hope, the most important relationship our children will have. Jesus said in Mark 12:30, 'Love the Lord your God with all your heart and with all your soul and with all your mind and with all your strength' and if our children are to respond to this commandment as we pray that they will, they will need us to teach them how to do it! Mum and Dad, are the ones who have the chance to teach them and show them by our example how to love, honour and respect God. That is quite a privilege but also a responsibility, because to have learnt these things properly will prepare them for a life-time of inner peace and satisfaction serving the one true and living God.

For our children then, to love and honour God will mean learning, in childlike ways, to do the things that we do as adult Christians.

They will need to become familiar with the Bible, knowing and loving the stories of the Old and New Testaments, holding in high regard all that God did for His people throughout History.

They will need to learn to pray which will sometimes mean sitting still long enough to concentrate on Him (though that's not to say that we can't pray while we're walking, running and playing as well) and also understanding that when we pray we must remember that the person we are talking to is the most important person in the whole world.

We will need to take them to church and help them know that the church is there as much for them as for the grown-ups. It is at church that they will see people worshipping and gradually experience doing it for themselves. If you are blessed in having lively children's worship at your church, this will happen easily. If not, you may need to be creative at home!

Our children will need to learn that to honour God is to value all that He has made — the world He has created and the people He has put in it. When we take care of God's world we are doing what God intended, after all when God made man he set him the task of taking care of the world and everything in it. Equally, to hold other people in high regard and care for them, looking outward rather than inward honours their Creator. We will look at this in more detail as this chapter unfolds. Similarly to care for the poor and needy honours God. Jesus said a time would come when He will say 'I tell you the truth, whatever you did for one of the least of these brothers of mine, you did for me' (Matthew 25:40). Whenever we make a sandwich for one of the homeless people who regularly come to our door, we always let the children take part, talking to them about what God says about caring for the poor.

Finally, we will need to remind our children constantly that all the gifts that they have come from Him and can be used for His glory and to honour Him. We are encouraging those of our children who are old enough to learn musical instruments and often talk with them about the possibility one day of using those musical talents to lead other people in worship. Similarly, our daughter loves little children and dreams one day of being a primary school teacher or similar. Sometimes we talk with her of using those gifts one day to teach children in a Sunday group. These things may never come to pass but the point is that our children are becoming aware that to use our gifts in God's service is a way of honouring Him.

Many of the things we've mentioned here will not come naturally! We will need to work at it but it is our firm belief that as we gently and prayerfully teach and encourage our children to honour God, it will gradually become a way of life for them.

2. Our children's relationship with Mum and Dad

The fifth commandment says this, 'Honour your father and your mother so that you may live long in the land the Lord your God is giving you.' (Exodus 20:12).

It seems that there is great blessing in store for those who not only obey (as we saw in chapter 7) but also honour and respect their parents.

Clearly God takes our relationship with our children very seriously and we, as loving parents, need to encourage our children to do the same. Of course respect has to come from the heart and will grow out of our relationship with them, but we can teach them gently but firmly how to honour us in practical ways.

The most important element of our children's relationship with Mum and Dad will be love and with that needs to come lots of fun and laughter together. When we talk about honouring Mum and Dad we're not advocating a return to the Victorian era where children were seen and not heard, and we're sure that wasn't what God meant either! It is so important to enjoy an open, warm relationship with our children in which they can come to us at any time, with anything on their hearts and know that we who love them unconditionally will always accept them and do all we can to sort out what's troubling them.

But it is quite possible for all of this to go hand in hand with an attitude of respect towards Mum and Dad. In fact, more than that, they are much more likely to come to us in this way if they have grown up to honour us and value our opinions.

What can we do, then, to help our children to live out this attitude of respect?

- Remember that God has called us to be parents not just 'friends'. This may go against our initial desire because we all want to be accepted by our children and to be "friends" brings real security. But to seek to be 'friends' confuses our children and implies an equal relationship which is not possible when you consider all the responsibility that we have as parents.

  This may be more difficult if you are parenting on your own because you may be tempted, as we said when we spoke about child-focused parenting, to share your problems with your child and perhaps allow your child to fill a void in your life. But God says in the Bible that children are to honour their parents. Letting your child be an equal may satisfy a short-term need, but in the end, when they are old, they may lose respect for your authority and standards and may even reject the relationship they have with you.

- Secondly, we can help our children to honour us by not allowing them to speak rudely to us or answer us back or boss us around, and by correcting them if they do. Sometimes it will come as a complete revelation to them that they were being rude by the way they acted or spoke. Just because we adults recognise rudeness it doesn't mean our children will and so we need to point it out gently. I remember once being very abrupt with our oldest child when she was rude to me and the next moment I looked round and saw that she was sobbing. 'I didn't know that was rude, Mummy', she said. Needless to say, I felt dreadful.

When our children are very young, before about the age of 3 while our parenting is typified by lots of 'no's' and 'don'ts' (see chapter 6) they won't understand the reason why they shouldn't shout at us or say 'no' to us. Our youngest child is at that stage and if she speaks rudely to me I tell her firmly 'You mustn't speak to me like that' or 'You don't say no to Mummy!' And if she resists she may need a stronger form of correction such as some time alone on the stairs.

But as they grow past about the age of 3 or 4, our aim is that they should move from not being rude to Mummy or Daddy because 'if I am I will have to sit on the stairs' to respecting us out of love for us and

desiring to treat us with respect. For our older children, then, it should be enough simply to explain 'the way you spoke to me then was not respectful' and as children who do want to respect us they will probably not do it again.

- Thirdly, there are practical things we can do to encourage our children to grasp the need to show respect and live it out in practice. Considerations like who sits at the head of the table at family mealtimes, or who sits in the front passenger seat of the car when the whole family is present. In our family, Mark and I generally sit in the front together and at either end of the table at mealtimes. Obviously there are exceptions for special treats or for everyone's convenience. But that is our general practice. Also, the children always ask us if they may have a drink, or a biscuit, or some more milk at the table or some of our writing paper to draw on. Generally the answer would be an immediate 'yes', but it is out of courtesy to us that we have encouraged our children not just to help themselves. As they get older, of course, some of these ground rules may change, but for the present it is a helpful practice for all of us.

A child's relationship with Mum and Dad is very important in this whole area of looking outward away from self. It's the closest relationship children have, certainly in the very early years and should be the one in which they feel most secure. It is therefore a very safe one from which to learn the attributes of honour and putting others first and how to express them, quite apart from the fact that this is God's plan for a child's relationship with his parents. With a little thought and effort on our part we can make it very easy for our children to live this out.

3 Our children's relationship with their brothers and sisters

In our own family, our children's relationships with one another are ones that we value very highly. There is nothing quite like having a brother or sister to play with, to share laughs with, to share tears with, to share toys with, and to help you learn to put others before yourself.

The Bible talks of brotherly and sisterly love in the book of Romans where Paul urges, 'Be devoted to one another in brotherly love. Honour one another above yourselves.'

Brothers and sisters matter and we need to work at seeing our children honouring one another above themselves. Also, our children's relationship with a sibling is often the first 'peer' relationship and if they can learn how to treat their siblings it will make other peer relationships so much easier to form.

So what can we do to help our children value their brothers and sisters and demonstrate that 'people matter' in this very special relationship in the family? Here are some of the things we do.

- We often refer to our children's siblings as 'your brother' or 'your sister' as a change from calling them by their Christian name. This is a good way of reinforcing the relationship for them and helping them to know what a special thing it is. Also we might often say things like 'isn't God good to have given you... as a brother or... as a sister?' This serves to remind them that a brother or sister is a great thing to have — someone who they will always be the best of friends with and therefore need to take care of!

- If we see one of them being kind to the other we try to praise them for it. This brings to their attention the fact that what they did was thinking of others rather than themselves and also encourages them, having received praise for it, to do it again next time!

- We encourage them to be glad when something good happens to one of their siblings and praise them when they manage it! Sometimes being glad for a sibling is hard, especially on birthdays when one person seems to be getting far too much attention for one day and it seems much longer than a year ago that you last had a birthday!

- Squabbles between brothers and sisters are inevitable but shouldn't be allowed to get out of hand. It is a very sad thing to hear brothers and sisters calling each other names or putting each other down. The Bible says in Proverbs (12:18) 'Reckless words pierce like a sword but the tongue of the wise brings healing.' We shouldn't underestimate the harm that can be done if a child is constantly put down by a sibling. And equally we shouldn't underestimate the good that can come from the carefully chosen words of a loving brother or sister. We encourage our children to be sensitive to one another's feelings, actively teaching them how to listen and respond to one another in a way that will build one another up.

- We encourage our children to be aware of the good qualities that their brothers and sisters have. Periodically during Family Time we ask the children what they especially like about each of the others and then we spend time thanking God for all those good things. This not only reinforces in our children positive feelings towards the others but also encourages each of them as they learn of qualities they didn't know they had!

If you are fortunate enough to have more than one child — and this is not something we take for granted as we wrote in chapter 5 — then your children have a wonderful opportunity for learning how to hold others in high regard and allow them to feel valued.

4 Our children's relationship with other adults

Children are very honest and what we see in their outward behaviour is often a reflection of what is in their heart. It is therefore all the more uplifting to be spoken to by a child who is happy to talk and has learnt how to esteem and value other adults in spite of the difference in age.

This won't necessarily come naturally. This came home to me all too vividly one day when I collected one of our sons from nursery. I found him chatting to one of the mothers and overheard this conversation. 'Are you James's mummy?' 'Yes, I am James's mummy.' 'Oh' said our son,' You don't look like his mummy, you look like his Granny!' Of course I was mortified but he had no idea why!

Obviously there are times when children will say the wrong thing in childish innocence and everyone forgives them for it. But there are also things that we can actively teach them to help them to make other adults feel honoured and valued. And it is down to us as parents. No-one else will teach them these things if we don't because we not longer live in a society where young people show respect to the more mature person by getting up to give them a seat (Leviticus 19:32) or holding the door open for them to go through first. But if we teach our children to do these things we are teaching them to look outward through the way they relate to other adults.

What can we do then to help our children to demonstrate respect for other adults? Here are some of the things we do.[1]

- We took time to devise some **family rules about what to do when an adult speaks to them.** Our children know that shyness is not an excuse for rudeness. We expect them to look an adult in the eye, say 'hello' and respond to their questions briefly. It's amazing what a difference it makes to a child's approach to an adult once they know what to do and say and why. You might even want to find something other than a Christian name for the children to use when addressing an adult such as Auntie or Uncle for family or close friends, or even something as radical as Mr or Mrs so and so. A number of people in our church, including ourselves, have adopted this and found it to be a helpful way of showing respect to adults.

- We teach our children **how to interrupt** us when we're in conversation with another adult in an acceptable way. It doesn't involve us immediately turning our attention from that person straight onto our child and communicating the message, albeit unintentionally, 'My child is more important than you. I must attend to him straight away.' (For the adult it feels a bit like when you're in a shop and the phone rings causing the assistant to break off from serving you to respond to someone who is apparently more important). So we've taught them to come and place their hand on our arm when they need to tell us something and to wait patiently. We can then place our hand on theirs to let them know we are aware of them and are waiting for a suitable break in the conversation to attend to them. Then we can ask them what they need. This lets everyone know, including our children, that other people matter and that we want to demonstrate that. Also it allows our children to communicate their needs to us, knowing they can trust us to meet them in an orderly way.

- We have always encouraged our children from an early age to write **thank you letters** for the presents they receive, as a means of instilling a sense of the value of others from the start. We want them to know that if someone has taken the trouble to send a present, then we need to take the trouble of writing to say thank you. For the very young ones we would write them ourselves, but from 4 or 5 they can easily dictate what they want to say. At 6 they could write one letter to photocopy and perhaps fill in the names and items and from about 7 or 8 they could probably manage to write most of their letters themselves.

- When we go to a **public place** such as a library or doctor's surgery or certain church services where people particularly need peace and quiet we have tried always to remind the children beforehand that there will be other people there who may have needs that are different from ours and we need to be mindful of that before we arrive.

- **Mealtimes** are always a great opportunity for teaching respect for others. To encourage our children to use good manners by not starting until everyone is served, saying 'please' and 'thank you', eating with their lips together and complimenting the cook rather than commenting unfavourably about the food are all ways of showing regard for those at the table, guests and family alike. Even the babies can use good manners. We taught our youngest child sign language so that she could say 'please' and 'thank you' and 'more please' and 'drink please' before she was able to speak. It made for much more peaceful family mealtimes!

5 Our children's relationship with their friends

What can we do in this age of competition and one-upmanship to encourage our children to value and esteem their friends and peers?

- Help them to be glad when something good happens to one of their friends. Every week on a Friday afternoon at our sons' school a shield is given out to the one who has been the kindest or friendliest to the other pupils that week. One day I overheard one of the boys excitedly telling his mother that his friend had won the shield that day. She said 'Oh that's wonderful, and did you all give him a clap?' Such a simple thing to say but it struck me then that she was encouraging him to be glad for his friend and cheer him on. That shield has a very special place in the life of the school and we are very thankful for that.

- Encourage them to respect their friends' belongings and at other people's houses wait until they are invited to play with the toys before they dive in. There is much in the Bible about private property (Exodus 20:15 'You shall not steal' is an obvious example) and it is important for our children to learn to take this seriously in relation to their friends' things, and also those of their siblings. We have tried to help our children to try to understand the value of things by allowing them to do little jobs to earn money. We're not talking about the household chores that everyone helps with but extra things, such as collecting all the litter from the front garden and receiving 1p for every piece they pick up. This is a great way of enabling them to save for things they want to buy and, we hope, teaching them the value of things because they have had to work for them rather than everything coming easily to them.

- Encourage them to look out for people who might be on their own in the playground and include them in their games.

- To the moan of 'It's not fair' that every parent must hear many times throughout their life, let them know that life isn't fair and help them to remember and be thankful for what they have, rather than what they don't have. Help them to see that to think of what we don't have will only make us discontent.

- Encourage them to pray for their friends and not just generally but for specific needs. Nothing will boost their faith more than for God to answer prayers for their friends.

- Encourage them to feel very honoured when they receive an invitation to a party. Tell them what a privilege it is to be counted as someone's friend. Have them make a card and wrap the present themselves

and maybe when they get a bit older pay a bit towards it. All of this will help to give them the feeling they are taking trouble with what they are giving their friend and may also help the friend to feel valued.

There is one final thing. We need to watch our example. Our children will be watching us to see whether we practise what we preach. So we need to ask ourselves how we treat our husband or wife, our close family, our friends and other adults. Do we take them for granted and talk about them behind their backs or do we encourage them and do things to show that we value them? Our children learn more from copying what we do in the early years than we realise!

So, what a wonderful opportunity we have to bring up our children to care for those around them and to do the right thing in their relationships with others. No-one would deny that it is hard work but with God's help we believe it's possible and the benefits are so worthwhile!

BIBLE VERSES USED IN THIS CHAPTER

Mark 12:31	Matthew 25:40
Philippians 2:3	Mark 12:30
Exodus 20:12	Romans 12:10
Acts 20:35	Proverbs 12:18
Leviticus 19:32	Exodus 20:15

Acknowledgements

1 Some of the ideas for valuing others were taken from *Growing Kids God's Way*, Copyright 1993.

Questions for discussion groups

1 Think about your own relationship with your parents. Do you honour them out of duty or devotion? Why?

2 How easily do we feel glad when something good happens to someone else? How can we seek to set a good example in this for our children to follow?

3 Do we live our life and encourage our children to live in a way that demonstrates the family value that 'other people matter'? How successful are we in this?

Application points...

1 Look out in your children for kindness shown to a sibling or a friend without being prompted and give them lots of praise.

2 Teach your children how to interrupt you respectfully and see how long it takes for your children to begin using it.

10

HOLD THE DREAM!

Over the last 9 chapters we have tried to encourage you to dream big dreams for your family, to have a vision for your family — and to believe that with God's help it is possible for that vision to become a reality.

We hope you have started to build up a dream for your family which you believe it is possible to achieve. Our prayer is that you have been inspired to make changes, to do things differently, to be proactive in making your family life even more fulfilling and pleasurable than it was before.

The thing about dreams is that you have to hold onto them. You have to work at making them come true. We want to encourage you to work at your dream until you see it come true. What can we do to help ourselves? The Bible talks in several places of the triad Faith, Hope and Love, three key things in our Christian walk. These three things are key in holding onto our dreams and visions for our families.

Faith

God is faithful and we can trust Him to take care of every aspect of our family life as we entrust it to Him. He will honour those families who seek to honour Him and as we prayerfully commit our ways to Him he will watch over us and guide us in our family life.

As parents who have a faith in God, that faith is central, to all that we do and it will be paramount that this faith is passed onto our children. We will want to be constantly teaching them about God and his ways but at the end of the day it will be our actions that will make the difference. Where our words are matched by life and action, our children will listen and learn from us.

Central to our Christian faith is the fact that through Jesus we have forgiveness of our sins. So sometimes we may need to say sorry to our children when we get it wrong. I know that I (Mark) can snap at my children when I am tired and I have to go to them to put the relationship right again. The point is that we have to model what we are saying. If we expect our children to say sorry to each other then it is important for them to hear Mum and Dad saying sorry to one another when things have gone wrong and for children to know that we will say sorry when we get things wrong.

God has given us His Word to help us in our parenting and we will need to have faith in His Word. We will always be bombarded about different ways of parenting with new ideas that might or might not work. Of course we should listen and weigh up the collective thoughts of the 'experts' but we need to have faith in what God has given us and not allow ourselves to be blown this way and that by the latest idea.

Have faith that with God's help you can build a better marriage. 'But my marriage is great' I hear you say. 'Yes, but it can always be better' would be my reply. Every year Lindsay seems to find a book from somewhere on marriage and I am given it for a birthday or Christmas. Reading new material and listening to other people's advice is always helpful even if we don't agree because it simply makes us more committed to the life we have chosen to lead.

Invest in your marriage. Take time for each other. Look for the good and the beautiful in each other. Stand

together with your mutual values and a common objective. Speak words of appreciation. Don't just find things to praise in your children but find things to praise in each other. Always have the capacity to forgive and forget. Don't be a historical partner, that is, one who always digs up the past, because you can bury a marriage with a lot of little digs. Look to the future, think how you would like it to be and then go for it. Often things are what we make them in life and if we invest in our marriages then we will have the best marriages on earth.

We believe that a marriage should have a honeymoon every year even if it is only for 24 hours. To take time away from the children and invest in the most important relationship in the home is crucial if we are to stay fresh and together in our parenting.

When investing in your marriage remember that it is not just about marrying the right partner but about being the right partner. Our marriages are what we want them to be. We have quite a large garden at home and every now and then we will spend a couple of days digging the flowerbeds, trimming the bushes and cutting the grass

and the garden looks great. It looks great because we have invested in it. Of course it doesn't take long for the weeds to grow back and the grass to grow long and the bushes to look messy again. The same is true of our marriages. We have to do a little each day to ensure that we live in love and peace together. If we invest in them, then the return will be great.

Have faith to believe that you are God's appointed parents for your children. Your children want to belong to your family. There could not be a better mum and dad for them. No-one could replace you as parents. God intended that you bring up your children. They love you as Mum and Dad more than anyone else. You are the best parents that they could ever have hoped for. To them you are the greatest. Build on this faith that they have in you. Don't give up working at your family identity. Work at ways of building on those God given relationships.

Have faith in your values. As long as our values come from the Bible then they are sure to be sound. In this *laissez faire,* feel-good world in which we live, many of your Christian values may well go against what the majority of people in our society uphold, but believe that they are good and try your hardest to stick to them. It's as we place the biblical values of honesty and respect and honour in our children's hearts and as we live them out in our lives that we will build a better tomorrow for our children's children.

Have faith in your methods of discipline. Consistency is so important. There will be people who don't agree with your way of parenting but there will be many others who do. Don't be tempted to conform to others people's views. You are the best parent for your child. Have faith in it. It's OK to say no to our children. It's OK to expect them to be considerate and to be polite. It's better for them to know what is acceptable and what is not because then they have great freedom within the boundaries that we set. Discipline helps our children to enjoy life.

And in the end we will have to have faith in God that He will have heard our prayers for our children. One of the hardest things that a parent is called to do is to let go. It starts happening as a child begins to go to school, then it builds over the childhood years until at some point they leave home. One of the most important acts of letting go is letting God be responsible for your child. Of course our praying never stops and we never stop being parents. However, our role changes to one of spectator as we watch our children find their own way in life.

Hope

Hope is a great thing. It allows us to stand firm in what we believe even when things around us seem grim. There will be times when, as families we go through hard times. No one escapes those, whether it be a bereavement in the family, a child being bullied at school, a teenager going through a lonely time, a redundancy, a family marriage break-up or something else. Very few people go through life without experiencing some kind of trouble. The important thing is never to lose hope. With God there is always a brighter future to look forward to and He will always help us through the darkest of times.

Hope is an integral part of being a parent. As parents we need hope. We hope that our children have caught our values. We hope that they will have found a mission in life. We hope that when our children are small we have instilled in them a sense of purpose, a thirst to make the best of all things and a desire to make a difference in this world. The question, 'What do you want to do when you grow up?' is so much more rewarding when it concerns not just economic activities but values and character and the contribution that your child wants to make to the future shape of this world. At our wedding in 1983 Bishop David Pytches said in his address, 'We all have the ability to shape the world we live in and Mark and Lindsay are choosing in Christian marriage to make this world a better place'. I remember thinking on the day, 'Yes, we can do something to make this world a better place'. I suggest that this is exactly the sort of vision or mission we want our children to have.

Of course we place into our children's hearts our values and beliefs. We place into their lives good things that will build them up and give them the best start possible. We pray for them and share with them our dreams for a better world and more loving communities. We hope that by the time they leave home that they too will be committed to changing the world. We hope that they will be committed to bringing up their children following God's guidelines.

Love

Our children need to know our unconditional love. This will mean laughing and playing and having fun and

adventures together. It is love that is accepting and yet guiding.

We live in a varied and diverse world. Our children face a noisy, image conscious, information-soaked, complex, over stimulating world full of challenges, opportunities, and choices. What we are seeking to provide at home is a place of security and love, a place where they know they will always be loved and looked after, a place where they can just be who God has called them to be, a place where they are allowed to fail as well as succeed.

This is the value that holds this book together: the value of love — a love that does not demand performance and always offers forgiveness. Parenting is such an exciting calling. It is the highest calling that we can have. God has entrusted us with lives to mould and shape. Into these lives we can place the unconditional love of God as well as our unconditional love. A love that seeks to build up and guide in right ways. It's a love that is not afraid to discipline for a better end.

It's a love that will commit you to start praying for your family. The testimony of many people who have done our course at St Paul's is that it has inspired them to start praying for their children and their children's future partners, if marriage is something God calls them to. In prayer we have this great and certain hope that God will hear our prayers and answer them. As we pray, so our children will pray!

Our love will be such that we will make time to be with our children. We are all faced with choices in life about how we spend our time and money. We urge you to choose, when it is possible, not to stay late at work and miss seeing your children. We urge you not to choose to watch a football match every Saturday if it means missing out on time with the family. One of my passions in life is playing golf and at one point I could play a reasonable game. However, with young children and one day off each week, golf is not a very family friendly activity. So I have had to come to the conclusion that I will now only play if I can book extra time off that doesn't affect my family too much. This means for me that I enjoy my game more because I know I haven't left Lindsay with all the children to look after and she can enjoy me playing.

With Faith, Hope and Love, in large quantities, our dreams for our families can come true. They really are within our grasp. And the exciting thing is that as we work at making our dreams a reality, we will impact not only our immediate families but we will also have an opportunity to change the shape and outlook of the communities in which we live and the churches we attend and the schools our children go to. If we provide our children with a model for parenting that is based on the Bible and that gives them a happy secure childhood and prepares them for tomorrow's world, then they will do the same for their children. But in addition, as others see what we are doing and begin to dream their own dreams and work at seeing them come true, we really will be making a difference to the society in which we live. We really will be doing something to make this world a better place.

Conclusion

Our aims in this book have been many. Perhaps the greatest aim has been to produce a book that is as practical as possible. We have attempted to provide a model for parenting that we have found helpful, which is based in the Bible. We hope that you will take what you can from it and apply it to your life and the lives of your children.

We hope that you have seen that the Bible has a great deal to say about parenting. To dismiss parenting as just 'down to chance' is a trap that many people fall into. We hope also that you will have seen that much of what we have written about parenting relates to our relationship

with God. Our own spiritual growth is not at odds with our parenting but will enhance it and be in harmony with it.

Our role as parents will not always be an easy one and just because we have read books doesn't mean that our children will be perfect. However I can say with confidence that we enjoy our children and I hope others do as well. All children have the potential to be a pleasure. We pray that all we have put over in this book will do for you and your children what it has done for us and ours.

If children live with criticism they learn to condemn.
If children live with hostility they learn to fight.
If children live with ridicule they learn to be shy.
If children live with shame they learn to feel guilty.
If children live with tolerance they learn to be patient.
If children live with encouragement they learn confidence.
If children live with appreciation they learn to appreciate.
If children live with fairness they learn justice.
If children live with security they learn to have faith.
If children live with approval they learn to like themselves.
If children live with acceptance and friendship they learn to find love — Anon

Bibliography

Shepherding a child's heart, Ted Tripp, Shepherd Press, 1995.

How to Succeed as a Parent, Steve Chalke, Hodder and Stoughton, 1997.

Growing Kids God's Way, Gary and Anne Marie Ezzo, Growing Families International, USA.

The Five Love Languages, Gary Chapman, Northfield Publishing, 1995.

The Sixty Minute Father, Rob Parsons, Hodder and Stoughton, 1995.

Loving Against the Odds, Rob Parsons, Hodder and Stoughton, 1994.

Appendix

RUNNING A FAMILY TIME COURSE

We hope that you will use this book to help you run your own Family Time Course. You will probably want to adapt it and use your own examples of family life before you present it. To get you started, here are some of the things we find helps the course run smoothly and successfully at St Paul's Ealing.

How long does it last? The course involves 10 sessions which can be run consecutively. Alternatively, we have found that it works well to have the sessions every other week. It then runs over a term and a half and gives people more time to think about the material between sessions. Also it feels less intensive in terms of time commitment.

Who should take part? Ideally if both parents are together the couple should do the course together. We have tried it both ways and the results are far more positive if both parents have taken part. Like us, you might think at first that this will put people off if their husband or wife isn't keen to do the course with them. But we have found that as we have persevered in encouraging couples to come together, the partner who was perhaps less keen initially has become committed and been glad that they signed up!

Obviously lone parents are welcomed with open arms and it's helpful to put them in groups with others in their situation.

Who should speak and lead? To lead a Family Time Course you will need to be seen to be living according to what you are teaching. We have had couples come and do our course at St Paul's who have then said they would like to go away and put it into practice for a year or so and then embark on running their own course. This may not be necessary as you may be doing all the things we talk about. You will know when you are ready. You will need to have a bit of experience of family life, so you won't be brand new parents, and ideally you will have children of various ages, the oldest one preferably being older or of a similar age to those of parents on the course.

What is the format of a typical evening? We begin at 8 pm with a welcome and notices and then we go straight into the talk. During the talk, people are encouraged to make notes on a note sheet that we hand out beforehand . After the talk we offer refreshments (tea and coffee with cakes which course participants bring on a rota basis each week). This social time is crucial and usually lasts about 20 minutes. After that we split into groups which are lead by a couple who we feel have leadership skills, have done the course previously and are seen to be living it out.

How many are in a group? Ideally we would have 4 to 5 couples plus two leaders. This gives plenty of opportunity to hear of others' experiences whilst not being so large that it intimidates discussion. It might be that you have only 4 couples doing the course, in which case you won't need to split for the group time!

What happens in the groups? In each session we would begin by asking the group to introduce themselves

- names and ages of children
- length of marriage if applicable
- occupation/interests
- church/organisations

- what each person hopes to gain from the course for them and their family

We begin each group session with a recap on the previous week, seeing how people have done with the 'application points' and answering any questions that have arisen. Then we have an open discussion following on from the talk we have just heard, using the suggested questions as a guide. We always close with prayer (for which we ask for requests from the families in the group), and this would be either open prayer or one of the leaders praying for everything, depending on the group make-up. As people leave we hand out a copy of the material we have presented that evening (for them to put in a course folder we provide) along with a sheet containing the 'application points' for people to work on at home.

Timing is crucial. It is important to start and end on time, particularly because the very nature of the course means that people will need to get home to relieve babysitters. 8 – 10 pm works well.

Babysitting Again, it's a good idea when writing to each participant to give them details of the course to include the telephone number of the Family Time venue. Parents need to be contactable and it will inspire confidence if they know you have thought of it ahead of time. It's worth saying too that in our church we have a Babysitting Ministry which has been set up especially to cater for courses such as Family Time and Alpha. A lack of babysitters can be a real hindrance to parents doing the course and if we can cross that hurdle for them, it may well be the deciding factor as to whether they come or not.

Photos About half way through the course we encourage everyone to bring photos of their children. By this time people have got to know one another and are itching to see pictures of the children they have been hearing about!

Final session In the final session the talk is shorter and we leave time for questions (which can have been submitted before the evening if desired) and for filling in a short questionnaire, a means of gauging people's response to the course. And rather than splitting into groups we have a longer social time with cheese and wine and nibbles.

Ongoing support We believe it is important for people to be supported as they seek to continue to work on their family life once the course is over. For those who are in our church this is easier but for those who come from further afield it is not so easy. We do try to encourage couples to link up and support one another and this often happens very naturally as people have made new friends through doing the course together.

In addition, we always arrange a course reunion about three months after the course has finished. We have tended to take over a local restaurant for an evening and come together for good food and a lot of fun.

We hope this is all helpful and will give you the confidence to run your own Family Time Course. It goes without saying that if you live near to Ealing and would like to join us for a course before setting it up in your own church you will be most welcome.

For more details call:

The Church Office, St Paul's Church, Ridley Avenue,
London W13 9XW
Tel. 0208 567 6717
Email: markmelluish@new-wine.org

New Wine Vision

Our vision at New Wine is to focus on what the Holy Spirit is doing and saying to the Church today.

New Wine Mission - So we seek:

- To exult the Lord Jesus Christ and to extend His Kingdom
- To listen to what God is saying through His Word and put it into action
- To co-operate with the Holy Spirit in envisioning the Church
- To prepare for Revival
- To model worship which is passionate, intimate, reverent and biblical
- To empower the people of God to move in the Gifts of the Spirit
- To encourage church planting
- To discern where the Spirit is leading in the areas of social responsibility, justice, the community and the environment
- To network with like-minded leaders across the nation
- We will endeavour to carry out this mission from the New Wine office by organising conferences and regional events, through our tapes, albums and videos, our New Wine magazine and a national New Wine network
- We will endeavour to do the same for young people through Soul Survivor.

New Wine Activities

Annual family and young people's conferences are held during August in Somerset, UK. In addition, training days, leaders days, leaders retreats, one-day conferences and regional events are held throughout the year. Conference booking forms and more information on our leaders' programme are available from:

New Wine, 4A, Ridley Avenue, Ealing, London W13 9XW.
Telephone/fax 0208 567 6717 Web Site www.new-wine.org